JULIA MUIR

T0124598

CHANGE THE GAME

THE LEADER'S ROUTE MAP TO A WINNING, GENDER-BALANCED BUSINESS

First published in Great Britain by Practical Inspiration Publishing, 2021

© Julia Muir, 2021

The moral rights of the author have been asserted

ISBN 978-1-78860-218-1 (print)
978-1-78860-217-4 (epub)
978-1-78860-216-7 (mobi)

The Ikigai Venn diagram was created by Marc Winn.

Practical Inspiration
Publishing

MIX
Paper from
responsible sources
FSC® C013604

For my mother Judy

The strong and supportive woman who is always there for me.
She was given few opportunities, but made sure I
was given many.

Contents

Part 2: The Six Steps to Success

Part 3: If not you, then who? If not now, when?

Foreword

I first came across Julia and her work as I was moving to the role of Chief Executive at Auto Trader Group plc. Our organizations had been working together for some time, but right from first meeting Julia, it was clear that she had huge drive and passion to make a difference to an industry that she had helped to shape over 30 years. Julia founded the Automotive 30% Club, a network of CEOs and managing directors aiming for a minimum 30% representation of diverse women in key roles by 2030. Auto Trader joined as a Patron member of the club as we shared Julia's passion to see more women promoted to leadership roles generally and specifically in the UK automotive sector. Our employees and members of our women's network have all benefitted greatly from the role models and examples that they have met at various events organized by the Automotive 30% Club.

At Auto Trader we have been on this journey in earnest now for over five years. We are one of the few FTSE 100 companies to have a board that is 50:50 women and men with an executive leadership team that is 40:60. However, the further we have come on the journey, the further we realize we still need to go because there are no quick fixes; it requires reworking of systems, processes and programmes at every level of the company. It starts with bringing the right mix of people into the organization at a graduate and early careers level, but also through returners programmes and later career guidance. Wherever they start from, we then need to continue this support as they move through the organization. We also place great focus on the importance of diversity within gender and acknowledge that the opinion of one white woman does not represent all women in our business. While we have more to do, there is no question in my mind that more diverse teams on the whole make better decisions and execute those decisions better, in no small part due to the 'richer collective intelligence' discussed in the book.

The debate surrounding women in leadership is not a new one. Some may even question whether we should have moved beyond this. However, it only takes a cursory glance at most leadership teams across most businesses to see that we still have a very long way to go. The mismatch between women in the population and in leadership positions is not something that we can or should accept. The problems are systemic and unless we take deliberate and potentially difficult actions, then we will find our organizations are no different in ten years' time.

That is why this book is so important, and few are as well placed as Julia to speak to the subject. Julia is the leading voice on gender balance in the UK automotive sector, a sector that has historically been seen as stereotypically male. This is somewhat ironic considering that a 2019 article in TI Media found that 90% of women have an influence on the household car purchase decision, and over 40% are the sole decision makers.

True to Julia's style, Change the Game provides a pragmatic, no-nonsense guide to the opportunity, the key issues and how we can all take action to solve them. Part 1 builds the case, providing evidence that gender-balanced teams produce better results and demonstrates how to become a more inclusive leader. In Part 2, Julia shares her Six Steps to Success, which provides a start-to-finish roadmap on how to achieve a more gender-balanced organization. Perhaps the most important section of the book is the final question to readers as to whether they will take their place in history by truly changing the game for the benefit of women, business and society.

I have met few leaders that don't believe in the value of diversity. What they often lack is the practical steps to do something about it, which is exactly what this book provides. For any leader looking to drive lasting change in their organization, this is a brilliant place to start. In the end, it is down to each of us to make a difference in our own teams and organizations. If we take up this challenge, we will not only do our part in creating a fairer and more equal society, but we will create better organizations for our people, customers and shareholders.

Nathan Coe, CEO, Auto Trader Group plc

About the author

Julia Muir is the CEO of the social enterprise Gaia Innovation Ltd, and founder of the Automotive 30% Club, a growing network of over 40 automotive-sector CEOs and managing directors aiming for a minimum of 30% representation of diverse women in key leadership roles by 2030. She has a business studies degree and a postgraduate diploma in human resource development, and is a veteran of the automotive industry with 30 years' experience in sales, marketing, organizational development and human resources. Julia has worked across the sector in retail, engineering, production and consultancy in Britain, Germany and Spain. During her employment at Ford Motor Company in the 1990s, she worked with Professor Jim Saker to create the BSc in Automotive Retail Management at the Loughborough University Business School Centre for Automotive Management, and later taught on their postgraduate diploma course from 2011 to the end of 2017.

Julia's primary goal is to help diverse youngsters and women achieve their full potential and overcome any impediments in their way. In this book, she explains the importance of finding your own life's purpose.

In 2016, Julia founded her business Gaia Innovation Ltd to build a positive ecosystem between schools, universities and inclusive employers in advanced technology sectors. Her aim is to inspire the next generation, particularly the disadvantaged, to seek rewarding careers in Fourth Industrial Revolution growth businesses and also reduce the UK skills deficit. During her schools engagement, she realized that youngsters are still constrained by gender stereotypes in careers, so she created a network of inclusive employer volunteers to raise aspirations and inform girls and boys that they have much broader choices. This ecosystem has now evolved into the Automotive 30% Club Inspiration for Innovation Network and aims to create an increased supply of diverse skilled employees in the future.

Also in 2016, Julia founded the Automotive 30% Club to encourage influential players in the sector to become inclusive leaders and build gender-balanced companies to achieve greater business success, thus also creating increased demand for diverse women. The name of the club was influenced by Julia's studies during her business degree of the work of Professor Rosabeth Moss Kanter, who observed that group dynamics change to be inclusive of a minority when that minority reaches a one-third representation level, rather than needing equal numbers. This led Julia to believe that the greatest energy must be put into reaching this tipping point, and once inclusion has broadly been achieved, equal numbers should follow. The percentage of 30% was chosen over the '33%' Club for brand aesthetics. When Julia discovered the Global 30% Club, established to increase diverse female representation in the FTSE 350 in the UK, she approached the then Chair, Brenda Trenowden CBE, who agreed to build a positive link between the clubs by giving the Automotive 30% Club the dual purpose of also being a working group for the UK Chapter of the Global 30% Club.

Julia advocates that organizations' working practices and cultures must be recalibrated to better suit the 21st-century worker and ensure diverse women and men will survive and thrive. She firmly believes that businesses are more profitable when both sexes work together in an ethical and socially responsible inclusive environment, and that gender equality benefits men as well as women. Julia provides advice to businesses on gender-balance issues and outreach activities. Her Gaia Innovation team run the activities of the club, which are sponsored by members and supporters, and in addition to the Inspiration for Innovation Network include the Inspiring

Automotive Women Awards, the Inspiring e-zine publication and Super-Network activities that motivate women to progress, and the annual Inspiring Automotive Women Day that connects female role models with hundreds of girls in primary and secondary schools.

Julia is a member of the steering committee of the Global 30% Club, a Gender Equality and Diversity Ambassador for the Silverstone Technology Cluster and also provides gender-balance and inclusion consultancy to construction companies. In 2018/19, she was the Private Sector Board Member lead on Employment and Skills and the Equality and Diversity Champion for the Sheffield City Region Local Enterprise Partnership.

Julia was listed in the FT and HERoes Champions of Women in Business in 2017 and 2018, and the HERoes Women Role Model Executives 2019 and 2020. She was also awarded the Mary Lou Carrington Award in 2016 by the City of London Worshipful Company of Educators for her work with the charity Speakers for Schools.

Introduction

At the time of writing in the summer and early autumn of 2020, the world seems to have been turned upside down. We're in the midst of a global coronavirus pandemic that by early October has killed 43,000 people in the United Kingdom according to official ONS figures (amended to only feature those who had tested positive within 28 days prior to death) and 213,000 in the United States. The US has erupted into civil rights protests across multiple states as a result of the death of George Floyd, and President Trump is following in the footsteps of the UK Prime Minister by catching the virus and suffering evident damage to his health, but also at a critical and potentially pivotal moment during the US election campaign. Unemployment levels are rising, the pandemic is widening the inequalities of race and gender, and UK businesses are being told to prepare for a Brexit future that's impossible to predict. We are entering uncharted territory and a new paradigm.

So against this backdrop of crisis and turmoil, I write to urge business leaders to use this burning platform, which is a moment of significant external impact and disruption to the status quo, to transform their organizations and maintain a focus on gender balance, women's inclusion and diversity. They can take their place in history by truly changing the game for the benefit of women, business and society. It is essential in a time of crisis to optimize business resources and work more efficiently and effectively. We must press the reset button now and take the opportunity to create a greener, smarter, fairer world for our lifetime as well as future generations.

Business teams with a balance of diverse women and men make better decisions than homogenous teams, leading to superior financial performance. This is due to their different but complementary insight, perspectives and propensity for risk. The rise in female purchasing power means that businesses with a better understanding of this customer will provide products and services with a broader appeal and so reap the returns in an economically challenging environment. We also know that the skills needed so urgently today, such as critical thinking, judgement and the ability to adapt quickly and pivot to new business models in a crisis, are found to a greater extent in inclusive teams. A gender-balanced diverse team is more important now than ever before.

In Chapter 1, I will outline the business case for higher diverse female representation in business. We must be mindful that women are still far away from having economic parity with men, impacting the wealth of the world as a result. McKinsey Global Institute in 2017 estimated that a whopping £150 billion would be added to UK GDP by 2025 if women participated equally in the economy.[1]

However, the report also stated that at the current rate we wouldn't achieve economic parity for at least 200 years, so reaching it by 2025 is a naive pipe dream. There's no doubt that the pandemic and the economic aftershocks are likely to stall this slow progression without radical intervention. The little progress made to date has resulted from huge step changes in societal attitudes such as equal pay and valuing the contribution of women in the workplace, along with scientific breakthroughs such as the contraceptive pill enabling women to work without employers assuming that at any point they would be 'incapacitated' by becoming a mother.

The shocking 200 years figure mobilized me in 2016 to personally take action to attempt to accelerate the pace of adoption of gender balance in business, in the firm belief that as well as improving business profitability it will also improve women's equality, social mobility and our society as a whole. I founded the Automotive 30% Club in 2016 to significantly grow the female representation in the sector by filling 30% of key leadership roles with women by 2030, and joined the steering committee of the Global 30% Club.

To achieve parity in my lifetime we must set out a robust plan to achieve it, understanding that the pace of change is usually exponential, and so reaching a critical tipping point of 30% may take the longest and be the hardest part of the journey. We usually overestimate what we can achieve in the short term and underestimate what we can achieve in the longer term. I believe the seismic shift caused by the rapid adoption of digitalization and remote working accelerated by the pandemic will enable inclusive organizations to reach this target earlier, and may lead to gender parity at least in many key roles in some businesses by 2030. In these companies, parity could be reached in ten years rather than 200, having a huge positive impact on the career progression of women and the carer opportunities for men.

Like the vast majority of women, I have experienced misogyny, sexual harassment, bullying and exclusion, and I would suggest that all women in the UK have suffered from at least one of these. I have had to curtail business events to travel home safely, be mindful of the clothing I wear and appease men who were making lurid jokes or telling me to smile. As a graduate intern at a car dealership, I've had keys thrown at my head by a male customer, and as a gender-balance campaigner I've been shouted at and had a finger jabbed in my face by an angry old senior male business leader who accused me of stirring things up.

However, I've also been lucky to have some brilliant women inspiring and guiding me. I've enjoyed the support of many fantastic feminists and am part of a large and growing team of mainly male leaders, advocates and allies who are running with the ball, have mobilized their people and are making huge changes to their organizational cultures and the profile of their teams. I firmly believe we can make the change happen.

This book walks you through the key issues surrounding gender balance and talks you through how to take action. In Part 1, I will provide evidence to support the business case for creating gender-balanced teams, explain the importance of inclusive leaders and how to be one, and urge you to act now because inclusive organizations are best equipped to manage the business transformation needed to weather the impact of the current multiple external crises. I assert that inclusive leaders are strong, are values driven and expect high performance standards, and show zero tolerance of the destructive forces of sexism, racism and homophobia in their businesses. I will show you how to create a perfect pitch to convince your team to be change makers and reduce opposition by dispelling the myths surrounding women's equality and positive discrimination. These should be replaced with facts and new legends to be passed on through your company. I explain the importance of removing unfair advantage by lifting up others and removing their impediments rather than disadvantaging the privileged, and talk about what both men and women can do as individuals to help the cause.

I will also share with you the secret of finding your purpose and reason for being, or Ikigai. This will lead to your fulfilment as a legacy-leaving game changer who will not only make a huge positive impact on the business but also on wider society.

My Six Steps to Success route map in Part 2 sets out a path to achieve a gender balance. The steps advise you to examine your data before jumping to solutions, identify female talent pools, recalibrate your practices and culture to ensure all good performers can thrive and adjust your recruitment processes so that they don't disadvantage diverse women. I also guide you through how to ensure women progress through the promotional pipeline and how to retain women in the business.

I use case studies from my Automotive 30% Club members to demonstrate the great work that is already being done by businesses today. I use the automotive sector as a microcosm of wider UK industry that since inception has been predominantly male. It has a stigmatized reputation for the undesirable characteristics that can result from a highly competitive macho culture, and I hope that by sharing the amazing changes that these automotive companies have already made, the practical applications can be noted and adapted for implementation in many other business settings.

Game-changing leaders create a compelling story to inspire others to adopt new norms. They implement new protocols to nudge people to adopt required behaviours and while leading the change from the top, they create change agents and champions at every level to drive the new ways of working. Now more than ever, it's essential to tap into the potential profits that your company might be missing out on and act to build a winning diverse gender-balanced business. In Part 3 of the book I reveal how to be a game-changing inclusive leader, and the importance of starting straight away.

This book will encourage, inform and give practical tips to those who know they must act to change the game now, and want to know how.

Part 1 Changing the game

1 The business benefits of balance: Don't settle for less

Businesses with a better gender balance are more successful, and employing more women in senior roles boosts financial performance for individual firms and the national and global economies. There is much evidence of this and every gender equality seminar and conference opens with citations to support it. It's not about a battle of the sexes, but an understanding of the benefits of balance; women and men working together achieve better results due to the different but complementary qualities and perspectives they bring, whether through nature or nurture, and combine to make better decisions. In this chapter, I will outline the broader business benefits of creating a business with values and achieving a more diverse gender balance. Marc Benioff, CEO and founder of Salesforce, succinctly summarizes this in the title for Part 1 of his book: 'Values Create Value'.[1]

More than a hundred years after women secured the vote in the UK, and 50 years after it was made illegal to pay women less than men, why are we still debating the benefits of employing the female half of the population in senior business roles? In contrast, we don't expend time and energy on arguing whether it makes business sense to employ men, or seek to justify that with evidence of enhanced performance for male-only teams (spoiler: there isn't any). In fact, there is evidence from studies of classroom behaviour that in predominantly male groups both males and females actually underperform. A quick google of 'business case for employing men' threw up no directly connected results, only those linked to gender-balance articles. In contrast, 'business case for employing women' gave 103 million results.

Why are we still discussing whether there is a place for women in leadership roles in business, and seeking justification for it on any grounds other than 'why on earth *wouldn't* we appoint women to top roles in 2020?'

You can rest assured that creating an inclusive culture and employing women in key decision-making roles will make your company more successful than if you only employ men in these jobs. The business case for the hiring and development of diverse women is supported by:

o Superior business profitability for gender-balance pioneers

o Profitability penalty for laggards

o Winning teams combine gender and diversity

o Improved customer insight and orientation

o Increased productivity and innovation

o Ability to attract talent

o Ability to attract investment due to effective and ethical decision making

Let's now examine each of these points.

Superior business profitability for gender-balance pioneers

Companies that address gender balance reap the returns. I am proud to be a steering committee member of the 30% Club, a campaign with a global mission to reach at least 30% representation of *all women* on all boards and C-suites globally.

On the 'Who We Are' page of the website, we make it abundantly clear that there is a robust business case:

> Gender balance on boards and in senior management not only encourages better leadership and governance, but diversity further contributes to better all-round board performance, and ultimately increases corporate performance for both companies and their shareholders.[2]

McKinsey & Company reviewed a 1,000-company strong dataset in 12 countries.[3] Their analysis published in 2020 found that companies in the top quartile of gender diversity on executive teams were 25% more likely to experience above-average profitability than peer companies in the fourth quartile. They also found that the higher the female representation, the higher the likelihood of outperformance. Companies with between 10% and 30% women are more likely to outperform those with fewer or no women executives, and those with more than 30% women on their executive teams are significantly more likely to outperform all those with fewer female leaders.

Earlier studies also found a strong business case for gender-balanced teams. An MIT study by Peter Dizikes found that professional services firms that switched from being all-male or all-female offices boosted their revenues by 41%.[4]

MSCI (an investment services firm) examined US companies with at least three women on their boards in 2016 and found that they had 10% gains in return on equity and 37% gains in earnings per share while those with no female directors had declines in both measures over a five-year period. MSCI found the same basic pattern in a global snapshot of companies in 2015.[5]

When Sodexo increased the number of women from 17% of the workforce in 2009 to 40% in 2015, it saw a 4% increase in employee engagement, a 23% rise in gross profit and brand image improved by 5%.[6]

There are many more sources of information providing evidence that businesses that are more balanced in terms of numbers of female and male leaders and, importantly, have reached a tipping point of at least 30% female representation, significantly outperform their peers.

Profitability penalty for laggards

We know there is a financial benefit to gender balance, but there is also a significant financial penalty relative to peers for tolerating a gender imbalance. McKinsey & Company's 2020 report identified a widening gap between those companies with the best and worst female representation, with a substantial performance differential of a huge 48% between the most and least gender-diverse companies. In 2019, fourth-quartile companies for executive-team gender diversity were 19% more likely than companies in the other three quartiles to underperform on profitability. This is up from only 9% in 2015, before the gender-balance pioneers started to break away from the pack.

McKinsey & Company also took a close look at the roles women occupy in the executive team. Only one-third of women executives in the 2019 dataset occupied line roles, with two-thirds occupying support or staff roles. Further, for companies in the bottom two quartiles for gender diversity, the proportion of women in staff roles is even greater. If more women could be employed in line management positions with the most direct influence on business performance and which provide a stronger path to the CEO position, there could be an even greater performance improvement.

Winning teams combine gender and diversity

Women comprise 51% of the population and are not a homogenous group. They have a range of ethnicities, cultures, ages and social backgrounds. Women are not all heterosexual and are not all mothers. When focusing on gender, it's easy to fall into the trap of picturing the female mirror image of the default white middle-class male on the board or on the executive committee, but we know that leadership teams with diverse members are more successful. When we aim for a gender balance, we must aim for it to be achieved through diverse women and men.

The 2020 McKinsey & Company report found a 36% higher likelihood of outperformance on EBIT margin for top-quartile companies for ethnic and cultural diversity on executive teams. Companies in the fourth quartile for ethnic diversity were 27% more likely to underperform on profitability than all other companies in the dataset.

The combination of a better gender balance and ethnic and cultural diversity, set within a carefully designed inclusive and cohesive culture, is a powerful one.

Improved customer insight and orientation

Intuitively, an organization that better reflects the market it is serving should have a better visceral understanding of the customer, and design products and services that meet the customer's needs better. Products are designed, engineered, manufactured, sold and maintained mainly by men, but bought increasingly by women. The rise of the female customer requires a company skill set and insight that understands and can serve the female customer better. Predominantly male teams will tend to design and deliver products and services that work well for men but not women. Apple made a famously expensive mistake by designing a health app that wouldn't work for women due to the physiological differences women have during their menstrual cycle. Women make up half of the health app market, yet the developers forgot women have periods. We can assume that if women had been properly represented on the team, this blind spot would not have occurred.

A joint 2019 report published by the Global 30% Club and PwC explains the potential missed profits from not doing business through a gender lens, and failing to tap into the vast and under-served female market.[7] There are huge gains to be made from ensuring women are not only attracted to your products through relatable marketing but can actually buy and use them effectively, through female-oriented product design, access to finance and access to the marketplace. To benefit from such gains, it's essential to have diverse women in your employee teams as well as in your supply and distribution chains.

There's still a prevailing attitude amongst marketers and investors that the women's market is 'niche', despite the rising numbers of financially independent women. It's widely reported that women make 70–80% of global purchasing decisions. Although I have been unable to find the original source of this claim, it resonates with most people that women not only shop for themselves but also make choices for the rest of the family. Women are therefore probably the largest consumer market, and products and services that appeal to them and meet their needs as well as men's will be more successful.

Organizations with customer-facing staff must take note that women may not feel comfortable shopping in all-male environments. From a young age, women are advised to be alert to the danger of predatory men (most of us don't tell our sons as a matter of course not to be predators and harassers, but we all tell our daughters that they must change their behaviour to avoid being the prey for someone else's son). Therefore, women will often intuitively avoid situations where they are likely to be either alone with an unknown man or significantly outnumbered by men.

The 2016 report by Different Spin – Good Rebels published the results of a survey conducted in the UK in collaboration with Netmums.[8] They found that only 13% of 48,345 women surveyed would dare to visit a car dealership unaccompanied. The car sales showroom seems to be the epitome of a stereotypical male environment within which many women, who influence the majority of car purchase choices, don't feel secure.

It makes sense therefore that organizations wishing to sell to women should create retailing environments within which diverse women feel comfortable and do not feel that they are a patronized or preyed-upon minority. A gender-balanced sales team would help to address this.

As the influence of progressive 'millennials' and the racial and gender equality activists of Generation Z grows, more customers will examine the equality credentials of the companies they buy from and will boycott those that don't match their values. Firms must look at their own leadership team and examine whether they are able to authentically do business with this value-based client base.

Increased productivity and innovation

Productivity is lower when there are fewer women in the organization. Hive, a project management software company, was able to anonymously source information from over 3,000 working men and women, and they revealed their analysis in their 2018 report on gender in the workplace.[9] They found that women were assigned 55% of the work compared to 45% for men, yet despite the 10% workload difference, both sexes completed 66% of their allocated work. The output for female office workers was therefore greater, showing that they are more industrious. Hive noted that women are assigned and spend more time on non-promotable tasks than men. These non-promotable tasks are any activity that is beneficial to the organization but does not contribute to career advancement.

A 2018 study by the Boston Consulting Group found that companies with more diverse management teams have 19% higher innovation revenues than those companies with below-average leadership diversity: 45% of total revenue versus just 26%, respectively.[10]

In a research study conducted in 2013 by Sylvia Ann Hewlett, Melinda Marshall and Laura Sherbin, leaders with different genders and diverse backgrounds and experience were found to help companies innovate more. Diverse leaders were more likely to create an environment where new and creative ideas were considered.[11]

The researchers scrutinized two kinds of diversity: inherent and acquired. They describe Inherent Diversity as involving the traits you are born with, such as sex, ethnicity and sexual orientation. Acquired Diversity is gained from experience: for example, working in another country can help you appreciate cultural differences. I can certainly support this from my own experience of working in Spain and Germany for several years. Prior to these assignments, when working in a role based in

Essex and responsible for marketing to customers across the larger European markets, I had been careful to equip myself with research and information about customers in those markets. I later realized though that all I had in my mind were stereotypical portraits of the people. Being immersed in the language and culture, observing and conversing with the people first-hand, gave me a much deeper empathy and insight into their needs and behaviour.

Hewlett, Marshall and Sherbin refer to companies whose leaders exhibit both *Inherent* and *Acquired Diversity* as having two-dimensional diversity. By correlating diversity in leadership with market outcomes, they learned that companies with 2-D diversity out-innovate and outperform others. Employees at these companies were 45% more likely to report that their firm's market share grew over the previous year and 70% more likely to report that the firm captured a new market. 2-D diversity unlocks innovation by creating an environment where 'outside the box' ideas are welcomed. When minorities form a critical mass and leaders value differences, all employees could have their ideas heard.

Most of the respondents, however, worked at companies that lack 2-D diversity in leadership. Without diverse leadership, women were 20% less likely than straight white men to win endorsement for their ideas; people of colour 24% less likely; and LGBT people 21% less likely. The researchers state:

> This costs their companies crucial market opportunities,
> because inherently diverse contributors understand the unmet
> needs in under-leveraged markets. We've found that when at
> least one member of a team has traits in common with the end
> user, the entire team better understands that user. A team with
> a member who shares a client's ethnicity is 152% likelier than
> another team to understand that client.

The positive results of diversity don't occur without psychological safety, however. People only contribute unique ideas to the group when they feel comfortable enough to speak up and present a contrarian view. Psychological safety is key to idea generation. Without it, even though women will have innovative ideas, they might hesitate to share them, and the opportunity to benefit from their creativity and insight is lost.

I will explain this need for inclusive leadership and creating safe environments further in Chapter 5.

Ability to attract talent

The most talented individuals are from both sexes and any ethnicity. They go to places that do better with diversity, and this may be what is driving diverse firms in certain contexts to outperform their peers as a positive upwards spiral occurs with diverse talent serving as a magnet for more diverse talent. In a survey of 1,000 respondents, the job site Glassdoor found that 67% of job seekers look at workforce diversity when evaluating an offer.[12] Top female candidates, in particular, care about gender-balanced work environments. Also, a 2017 survey by PwC found that 61% of women look at the gender representation of the employer's leadership team when deciding where to work.[13]

It's not financial success that attracts women to companies; it's women that help the company to succeed. In research published in their 2019 *Harvard Business Review* article, Stephen Turban, Dan Wu and Letian Zhang didn't find evidence that high-performing teams simply attracted more women; they found that hiring more women in the team led to the higher performance *after* they were employed.[14]

Millennials are now leading our businesses at senior and middle management, and have notably more inclusive values than those they have succeeded. Generation Z are entering the workforce and many are already actively supporting gender and racial equality movements. Deloitte's 2018 *Millennial Survey* found that these employees seek diversity, and it is undoubtedly the case that they seek out inclusive employers with diverse leadership teams and will not settle for companies with outdated values and working environments.[15] Deloitte's 2020 follow-up survey with millennials also found that job loyalty rises as businesses address employee needs, from diversity and inclusion to sustainability and reskilling. For the first time since the survey in 2016, the majority of respondents said they would stay with such employers for at least five years rather than two.[16]

Ability to attract investment due to effective and ethical decision making

Many investors now look at gender and diversity within a company's leadership as an indicator of effective and more ethical decision making and leadership, which in turn is an effective predictor of future performance. In addition to all the factors that lead to the superior performance of heterogeneous teams already listed, homogeneous male boards and executive teams can fall into the trap of 'group think', being complacent and not spotting threats, or turning a blind eye to unethical behaviour to ensure other goals are met. Or they can be overconfident and make riskier decisions because no one questions their validity or provides a counter perspective.

There are many examples of powerful all-white male boards making risky and unethical decisions and setting a culture that normalizes unacceptable practices. Back in the early 1970s, Ford Motor Company in the US found their Pinto car had a design fault that was a fire hazard. It was later revealed that the company concluded that the number of likely deaths and amount of required compensation would be lower than the cost of redesign, and so didn't address the fault. Lee Iacocca, the CEO at the time, had famously said: 'Safety doesn't sell', sending a strong message about company values. However, the modern Ford Motor Company now has three women and ten men on the board, and has long championed diversity, inclusion and ethical decision making.

A CMI report published in March 2014 revealed the findings of research conducted amongst CMI members across private, public and not-for-profit sectors through the completion of an online profiling tool.[17] They found that, on average, female managers score 5% higher than men on the ethic of care at work, underlining the added value they bring to leadership and board roles.

Working to achieve a gender balance and diversity is now seen as good governance. The Hampton-Alexander Review monitors the female representation of women in senior roles in the FTSE 350. Their 2019 report emphasizes the link between diversity and governance:

> *The new corporate Governance Code rightly reinforces the importance of succession planning. The code puts diversity at the heart of good governance, requiring Nomination Committees to link their policies on diversity and inclusion firmly to their business strategy and to promote diversity in terms of new appointments and in their succession planning. As companies apply the new code in 2020 they will be expected to demonstrate how they have sought the right mix of skills and perspectives to drive their long-term success.*[18]

In addition, they claim that investors are increasingly considering diversity a voting issue and examining whether they can support individual director re-election at company AGMs. In 2019, 30 companies' nomination committee chairs and 30 board chairs featured on the Investment Association's Public Register have experienced significant shareholder dissent. Investors are holding these individuals responsible for ensuring the board is governed well and prioritizing diversity.

Summary

There is overwhelming evidence that businesses perform better when they include women, and even better when the women are diverse. This is due to the more effective decision making and higher level of collective intelligence that stems from a team with wider perspectives, broader experiences, complementary characteristics, ethical governance and a balanced approach to risk.

So if your leadership team is currently all male and homogeneous, you really are settling for less. Change that.

It is clearly not as simple though as 'hire more women – get better results'. It's essential to purposefully design an organizational culture and structure that optimizes the contribution of both women and men of all ethnicities, to optimize results. This is achieved through inclusive leadership, the subject of the next chapter.

2 Inclusive leadership: Create a winning business

Diversity leads to better performance, but not always. Diverse people must be connected into a cohesive balanced network through inclusive leadership, with a common purpose and shared company values. It's not simply about having diverse men and women, but the right men and women to work together well. Complements must overlap to ensure a shared understanding and common ground. For gender to increase group performance, you need team members with different perspectives to add value. Diversity without protocols to create cohesion could actually hurt team performance due to competition and conflict.

To reap the benefits of gender balance, you must ask yourself: 'Am I an inclusive leader?' Truly inclusive leaders have strong personal values, a high degree of self-awareness, are open and transparent, set a high standard for performance and ethical conduct, and weigh up multiple viewpoints before making decisions, appreciating collective intelligence. Being inclusive is not enough; they also actively avoid excluding any person who could make a positive contribution to the business. As Nathan Coe, CEO of the FTSE 100 company Auto Trader notes, 'It's as much about the battle against exclusion as it is about inclusion.'[1]

In this chapter, I will explain the importance of inclusive leadership in your organization. Business in the Community (BITC) define inclusive leadership in their 2011 report as 'a leadership style which embraces, encourages and taps into the creativity and ideas which come about in non-homogeneous groups'.[2] Their survey found that 84% of respondents with an inclusive leader said they felt more motivated; 83% said they had increased loyalty; 81% reported that their performance and productivity had improved; and 81% reported that they were motivated to go the extra mile above and beyond their day-to-day role.

The BITC report describes inclusive leaders as pioneers, adaptable to change, with a high level of diversity awareness. They use new and flexible approaches to organizing work to get the best results. Inclusive leaders are skilled at adapting their style to complement the contribution of others, and respect different cultural perspectives. They foster innovation because employees feel safe, valued and empowered to innovate in a culture that rewards trying even if it leads to failure. Skilled in building a diverse talent pipeline, innovative leaders personally seek out and support the development of the best talent from a range of backgrounds.

Inclusive leaders design a winning business by focusing on relationships with people (employees, customers, investors and the community) and will:

o   Identify and embody core values

o   Understand the difference between diversity and inclusion

o   Create an inclusive culture

o   Design the organization for inclusion

o   Avoid exclusion

Let's explore these characteristics further.

Identify and embody core values

An inclusive leader identifies the core values that will build a winning inclusive business, designs an organization around them, and sticks to them. Marc Benioff, the founder and CEO of the highly profitable CRM solutions company Salesforce, is a good example of an inclusive leader. In his 2019 book, he claims that equality is one of the core values of his company, along with trust, customer success and innovation. He points out that these all create value for the company in different ways, but are also intertwined: 'They work together to create the momentum that keeps our flywheel spinning.'[3] He also states: 'Holding equality as a value is not just a matter of fairness, or doing the right thing. It's a crucial part of building a good business, plain and simple.'[4]

In the early 1990s, I was an Investors in People consultant and assessor. I would advise businesses of all sizes and sectors about the benefits of putting people first, and how to create cultures and design structures to optimize employee engagement. I was able to accurately assess an organization's culture within a few minutes of entering the workplace through simple cues: the language used on notices, the number of hierarchical management levels in the org chart, the formality of the dress code, the homogeneity of the faces, the buzz of enthusiastic and friendly productivity or the hush and lowered eyes of subordinate employees in an autocracy. The meeting with the owner or CEO would seal my intuitive assessment of the culture because the person would usually embody it.

One of the warmest, gender-balanced cultures I experienced was that of Bettys and Taylors Group of Harrogate, a family-owned business behind Yorkshire Tea, Taylors of Harrogate coffee and Bettys Café Tea Rooms. Their values were the Six Ps: Prosperity, People, Planet, Product, Passion and Process. Female and male employees felt valued and included and were very engaged. Ten years later, I travelled from my home in Essex to Harrogate to collect my bespoke wedding cake from them because I trusted it would be perfect (and it was). A quick look at their website shows a thriving company, with a board of four women and three men and an intriguing organizational structure showing a 'collaborative CEO' group of one woman (who chairs the group and also sits on the board) and four men. Their 2019 gender pay gap report shows an impressive 48% female representation in the top quartile and 42% in the upper-mid quartile. Although it's clear that there is little racial diversity in the company (Harrogate's population is 97% white), their Twitter account for Yorkshire Tea responded to an openly racist woman: 'Please don't buy our tea again. We're taking some time to educate ourselves and plan proper action before we post. We stand against racism.'[5] It is clear that the company is still firmly sticking to its values and inclusive culture and has a much better gender balance at the top than most.

Understand the difference between diversity and inclusion

It is frustrating to see the terms diversity and inclusion often used interchangeably when in fact they mean different but complementary things.

Diversity describes what you need in order to develop a richer collective intelligence: a wide range of different female and male employees with varying experiences and perspectives. Some people are diverse in multiple ways, with intersectionalities between gender, ethnicity, sexual orientation or disability. A report by The Diversity Practice in 2007 explored the successful traits of a number of high-achieving BAME women. They found that the women have 'bicultural competence', being familiar with both British values and the norms of their ethnic group, giving them the ability to manage and lead across cultures. This cultural breadth and learning, from the challenges and experiences they have faced because of their race and gender, also gives them the ability to see things from multiple perspectives and often come up with novel solutions to problems.[6]

Inclusion is how you effectively integrate such diverse people into a team to ensure that the sum is greater than the individual parts. If you don't establish an inclusive culture to enable the people to work in a manner that complements the different skill sets, respects differences and identifies common ground, then heterogeneous teams can suffer more internal conflict than homogeneous teams. So it's not just important to have a diverse team; you need to have an authentic diversity climate that is inclusive and doesn't exclude people.

Create an inclusive culture

Joep Hofhuis, Pernill G.A. van der Rijt and Martin Vlug found in their research published in 2016 that a diversity climate, defined as an organizational climate characterized by openness towards and appreciation of individual differences, has been shown to enhance outcomes in culturally diverse teams.[7] They suggest that a perceived diversity climate in an organization positively relates to job satisfaction, sense of inclusion, work group identification and knowledge sharing in teams.

I see a successful business culture as demonstrating the norms of a vibrant network, holding together an interdependent and balanced ecosystem of people with varying backgrounds, experience, expertise and perspectives. Just as in any other network, power comes from the strength of the links between the different nodes rather than the nodes themselves. Inclusive leaders create successful companies by building strong links between diverse people, integrating them harmoniously into a culture that supports the contributions of all people. This positive culture leads to employee engagement, and grows when the organizational structure and processes facilitate it through clearly articulated and shared values, positive behaviour, effective communication channels, clear roles and responsibilities, and fair and transparent promotion and reward policies. Such productive conditions result in superior performance.

A truly inclusive culture cannot exist without women, and a gender balance will never be achieved without an inclusive culture. The ecosystem creates the conditions necessary for women to thrive and for achieving and maintaining a gender balance. Without diverse women, the ecosystem cannot be balanced and inclusive. Diversity in itself does not automatically lead to inclusion or superior success; inclusive leadership is required to create the balanced ecosystem.

Design the organization for inclusion

It's important to consciously design the organization for equality so that it actually becomes too much like hard work for individuals to uphold inequality. You may never be able to change ingrained attitudes and you are not the thought police, but you can change behaviour in your workplace through redesigning the environment and ways of working so that new norms emerge. What companies live and breathe matters, more than any written corporate codes of conduct. Celebrating and rewarding the desired behaviour, and building in protocols that minimize the exclusion of anyone, are more effective than detailed policy manuals that no one reads. Promote behaviours by harnessing people's desire to imitate, compete and gain social approval. Use rules, laws and codes of conduct to simply then express and explain these norms.

Many companies have introduced unconscious bias training but I'm afraid the jury is still out on whether it has the desired effect. Some researchers believe that making people aware of their biases can actually make it worse.[8] It's wiser to help people to realize the advantages they may have personally over others, eliminate the impact of bias by designing processes that prevent it happening, calling out micro-aggressions, role modelling good behaviours and nudging behaviour in the right direction through peer pressure, so that people simply no longer manifest their bias through their actions.

Lockheed Martin has embraced an inclusive approach for several years. Leaders from top and middle management attend development training to explore the uncomfortable issues of bias and exclusion in the workplace and to build empathy and understanding, and foster a working environment that is equitable, productive and inclusive. This gives them insight into how they may have benefitted from their gender, class or race, rather than their innate ability, to get to where they are. The teams of leaders that have participated report higher levels of inclusion, engagement and trust than teams of leaders that haven't gone through training. This programme gives people a broader perspective and appreciation of others rather than focusing on any biases they may have.

Avoid exclusion

Inclusive leaders are highly aware of diversity amongst the people they work with and manage, and are aware of gender and cultural differences. A leader can't claim to simply be blind to gender or ethnicity. This would actually make women and people of colour and their lack of representation invisible, and can lead to them being inadvertently excluded. The person actually becomes blind to the fact that there aren't any leaders other than white men, and doesn't question why this would be.

As a business leader who wishes to build a successful winning business by tapping into the superior collective intelligence, experience and expertise of a diverse group of people, you can't be ambiguous about sexism, racism and homophobia. It's important to acknowledge that most people, including me and you, are to greater and lesser degrees unintentionally prejudiced against others who are not like ourselves due to our socialization since childhood. But most people will do all they can to avoid behaving with prejudice and will actively try to be inclusive. However, sadly many people choose to be racist, sexist or homophobic (and often the three go together) and truly believe that women and people of colour should not be afforded equal opportunities. Some people believe that they have succeeded solely due to their own abilities, ignoring that they have enjoyed significant advantages over others, by being male or white, or both. As organizations begin to take action to create a level playing field and ensure fairness is applied by removing unfair barriers in the way of women and people of colour, they feel threatened by competition that previously didn't exist.

However, as an inclusive business leader you and your leadership team must be clearly anti-exclusion, and show zero tolerance of racism or sexism in your organization. You cannot employ an individual who views others as lower-status beings if you are building inclusive teams; so in that way, there will be a natural limit to whom you wish to include in your business, and to whom you wish to sell to. You must decide the culture you wish to create in the organization and make the company values of equality and respect transparent to all. Zero tolerance of sexism and racism should also be extended to suppliers and contractors, and they should be encouraged to adopt similar inclusive values to your company to deserve your business. This is not about being 'woke' or 'politically correct'; it's about ensuring others are treated the way you would wish to be treated. This is essential for building winning teams that perform to their full potential because every individual's contribution is unhindered, optimized and visible.

Where better to look for guidance on this than Chancellor of Germany Angela Merkel, the leader of a country that uniquely knows the dangerous consequences of exclusion. In her passionate speech to the German Bundestag on 27 November 2019, she exclaimed: 'Freedom of expression has its limits. Those limits begin where hatred is spread. They begin where the dignity of other people are violated.'

Summary

The positive effects of inclusive leadership lead to the superior financial performance of diverse gender-balanced companies that include women as decision makers. To be an inclusive leader, you must lead by example and role model the required behaviours.

I've observed that companies already reaping the benefits of female representation are led by bosses with inclusive leadership characteristics. They have created cultures and designed working practices to secure the optimal contribution of all team members and to actively avoid exclusion. Although these pioneering leaders naturally embody these traits, I believe that inclusive leadership can be learned and adopted by others once they understand their importance in achieving business success. It's not something that can be delegated to HR or the diversity and inclusion manager; successful leaders must embody inclusive behaviour themselves.

As Nathan Coe, CEO of Auto Trader Group plc, observes:

> It's people like me who need to go on this journey. It's not ok, whether talking about race or gender or sexuality, to just hand over to those groups and say 'why don't you make us more inclusive?' It's people like me that set policies, set norms, set accepted social behaviours that really need to get to grips with this. My journey has been very humbling because you do start to realize how much you don't know about the world and the experiences people have.[9]

If you are an inclusive leader or want to be one to successfully run a winning gender-balanced business, for the reasons outlined in the following chapter, now is the time to take action.

3 A burning platform: Now is the time

We've learned that organizations with female and ethnic minority representation in the leadership team make better business decisions that lead to superior performance relative to their more homogenous peers, due to their complementary perspectives. We know that the skills needed to employ critical thinking and balanced processing, and to adapt quickly and pivot to new business models in a crisis, are found in inclusive and diverse teams. The increased purchasing power and influence of women over the last few decades has also made it clear that businesses with a visceral understanding of their customer base would intuitively provide better products and services and so reap the returns in an economically challenging environment.

This chapter will outline why now is the time to act to transform your business.

As a leader, you are currently standing on the burning platform of a turbulent business environment. The flames are coming from multiple scorching points, resulting from the commercial world in the UK being impacted by four potentially cataclysmic events that are hitting almost simultaneously:

o   The skills deficit due to digitalization

o   2020 COVID-19 pandemic

o   The 21st-century fight for racial equality

o   Brexit

It's clear that the combination of these events has created a perfect storm, leading to the reorganization of skills, the rethinking of values and the digitalization and recalibration of processes on a huge scale. Arguably it has never been more critical for a business to 'change or die'.

This burning platform is leading many companies to innovate and transform rapidly and look to new and historically untapped sources of skills. They are looking to embrace the change necessary to recruit diverse women, and in so doing close the skills and gender gap.

You need to act now to build a winning gender-balanced team. Now is not the time to lose faith or scale back your plans for inclusion; for any or all of the following reasons, it's needed now more than ever before.

The skills deficit due to digitalization

The key challenge faced early in 2019 by Industry 4.0 growth sectors was a deficit of the skills needed to drive transformation swiftly on a large scale. Industry is undergoing rapid digitalization. Technological advancement is occurring at an accelerating pace, driven by a number of key trends: the climate change emergency leading to a goal of zero emissions and a step shift to sustainable energy; the move towards 5G, autonomous vehicles and smart cities; social trends leading to changes in purchasing, ownership and usage models; the introduction of digitalization and automation to improve productivity and efficiency; and the harvesting and use of big data.

This business transformation can only be achieved through people, but there is a huge skills deficit in most industries and the race is on to attract people with new skills from different sources. This is highly competitive, because all Fourth Industrial Revolution growth sectors (including construction, engineering, automotive, aerospace, health and digital technology) have large skills deficits. Employers are looking for digital technology skills, but also design flair, creativity and advanced engineering, as well as a high level of commercial acumen. They need innovative thinking, critical analysis and balanced decision making, as well as emotional intelligence and enhanced personal and social skills.

PwC's annual survey of global CEOs in 2017 revealed that the most important skills required to respond to a rapidly changing business landscape were problem solving, collaboration, adaptability, leadership, emotional intelligence, creativity and innovation.[1] Many of these skills had not previously been seen as the traits of a successful leader within predominantly male organizations, and so are now being actively sought from more diverse sources. The need for these human skills is now also combined with data analytics, and their scarcity has been echoed in the survey in every subsequent year.

By 2019, transformation of the business environment leading to skills shortages was a burning platform significant enough in its own right to drive change. Companies on a growth trajectory in the traditionally male-dominated technology, engineering, construction, manufacturing and automotive sectors were forced to embrace the change necessary to attract, recruit and retain from the female talent pool, and in so doing close the skills and the gender gap. They simply would not be able to grow without doing this. Gender-balance experts were finally being invited to speak at conferences in recognition of it being a core business imperative.

And then the pandemic hit.

2020 COVID-19 pandemic

On 12 January 2020, the World Health Organization confirmed that a novel coronavirus had caused a respiratory illness in the city of Wuhan in China, which then spread to all provinces of mainland China. The first cases in England were identified in late January, and the number of cases increased rapidly in March, resulting in a UK-wide 'lockdown' on 23 March that was then lifted gradually in phases between May and July.

At the time of writing, the Office for National Statistics had officially confirmed over 43,000 deaths within 28 days of a positive COVID-19 test result, and measures are again being reintroduced in many regions to restrict social gatherings as infection rates have started to rise once more.

Economic health is now in question, with experts comparing the effects of the pandemic, lockdown and subsequent changes to consumer behaviour to the recession of 2008, the crash of 1929 and the post-Second World War period. Workforce ability and resilience play a key role in how the nation weathers this storm, and we are moving to a phase where collective employee health or sickness may correlate to that of the economy. The impact on skills, as an all-encompassing term for building and leveraging capacity, capability and coordination, is potentially far reaching, affecting UK needs right now and in the years to come.

Many thousands of people are being made redundant as they emerge from furlough, because businesses have accelerated labour-saving automation and digitalization, or need to cut costs to survive, or have actually failed. Many of the hardest-hit sectors are those with customer-facing business models and have predominantly female staff, such as hospitality, retail and entertainment. It's therefore expected that women will be disproportionately affected by the downturn. As schools open their doors again with strict measures to prevent mass infection, many children are being forced to self-isolate if a peer develops symptoms, leading to childcare challenges for working parents. As the burden of childcare currently falls disproportionately on women, juggling unpredictable school absences with work could endanger their employment prospects in such a volatile labour market if their bosses do not take action to retain their skills for the long term.

The class of 2020 school leavers, having had their education curtailed and having suffered exam results chaos, will lack work experience and internship opportunities that are so important for developing employability skills. Companies forced to downsize will freeze their apprentice graduate recruitment, thus missing out on the opportunity to rebalance gender representation at the entry levels and leaving a cohort of youngsters in limbo.

The pandemic has become an existential threat to business growth, and companies have been rapidly forced to pivot to serve new customer markets, move to online selling and embrace remote working. It has brought to the foreground the need for a high level of personal skills, particularly resilience and the ability to embrace change and be adaptable and flexible in the fluid commercial landscape. More than ever before, a diverse gender-balanced high-performing team is critical to be able to respond swiftly and effectively to the crisis and the future commercial landscape.

I have observed that inclusive leaders are weathering the storm of the pandemic. They are putting the safety of people first, showing empathy for employees and customers, innovating with new processes and agile working, and collaborating with peers, partners and clients to develop long-term solutions that are improvements on the past. Many have continued to pay furloughed workers their full pay, and are also going beyond their statutory obligations and providing enhanced sick pay to those falling ill, as well as checking in on their mental wellness. They are listening to their staff and ensuring that women are not being adversely affected more than men due to events beyond their control. Many are prioritizing a return to the office for young workers who find remote working difficult due to accommodation or mental wellness reasons, and enabling those with families to work productively from home.

Their teams will avoid burnout, stay healthier and resilient through the second wave, and their businesses will continue to function successfully through the new normal. By keeping a focus on gender balance and inclusion, they will avoid losing talent and will be better equipped to find innovative solutions to overcome future shocks.

It could be argued that the negative impact of the pandemic on the economy and the expected high rates of unemployment might ameliorate the skills shortage and so stall the gender-balance movement. However, in my discussions with inclusive business leaders it has become clear that those earmarked for redundancy in their companies are those who don't have the skills revealed to be so critical in the challenging pandemic period, or the willingness to develop them. They may be in roles that are now doomed to become obsolete due to the accelerated adoption of automated systems and online selling through lockdown, and have not been able to embrace the change and swiftly develop the skills necessary to be moved into another role. There is a huge mismatch between supply and demand and the search for the skills for the new way of working is still on. These people are not being displaced due to their need for flexibility or remote working; in fact, that is sometimes seen as a positive, and so women are not being made redundant in greater numbers than men in inclusive organizations. The minority that are the underperforming, intransigent and inflexible people of both sexes appear to be at most risk during this period of transformation.

Inclusive leaders will create the right environment for diverse people to thrive, but will also rigorously enforce the requirement to perform, contribute and be productive. Those who cannot deliver to the required level will be managed out of the business. It will still be necessary to search for candidates with the right skills to drive the business forward, but through a tsunami of unsuitable displaced applicants.

And then in the middle of the pandemic period came 'Black Lives Matter'.

The 21st-century fight for racial equality

The killing of George Floyd by a Minneapolis police officer in May 2020 triggered a shockwave around the western world. Filmed by a passer-by, the distressing footage showed the officer kneeling on George's neck, ignoring his exclamations that he couldn't breathe, until he died nine minutes' later.

In the midst of a global pandemic, people across the US and Europe marched under the banner of 'Black Lives Matter' (BLM) in protest at the disproportionate number of deaths in police custody and arrests of black people in the US, and are shining a spotlight on similar events in their home countries. However, support for the (sometimes violent) protests was far from universal, and was followed by a wave of protestations that 'All Lives Matter', revealing the refusal by many white people to acknowledge their position of relative security, and also unleashing a tide of openly racist comments on social media. This made it clear to many inclusive leaders that it's no longer sufficient to declare that they're not racists; it's now important to declare they are anti-racist and will take a stand against any form of discrimination, supporting the right to peacefully protest while condemning violence.

Many companies wrote to their employees or took to social media to commit to an anti-racist stance and to communicate that racism would not be tolerated in their organizations, or in their local communities. Others stated that they would do better to ensure there was no discrimination or barriers faced by black, Asian or ethnic minority populations in their companies and to ensure better representation. This signified an important change in mindset from what has been historically a passive 'sitting on the fence' tolerance of racism, or an internal approach to addressing racial equality, to taking an active stance to fight racism in the outside world.

This route to racial equality follows a similar pattern to gender equality; the battle for equal treatment, opportunities and representation has been fought by women and their allies for over a hundred years. Women of colour have battled on both fronts. There are many people in positions of power in business and in politics who still believe that a woman's place is in the home and that she is not capable of matching a man's abilities. Many advocates of gender equality and diversity have been told that it is positive discrimination or unfair to men (as with the 'All Lives Matter' banner expressing a sentiment that BLM is unfair to white people), or have been told that barriers to progression faced by women and ethnic minorities simply don't exist any more.

As an inclusive employer, you can't sit on the fence. Your goal is to build a team from the best-performing highly skilled people you can find, and these high performers will include a diverse range of women from all ethnicities. You must ensure your organization is an environment in which they can thrive; and show zero tolerance for the people who demonstrate through their words or behaviour that they don't wish them to succeed based on innate prejudices against their gender or skin colour. Women of colour and their allies, particularly amongst the talent pool of highly educated millennials, will check out the diversity credentials of future employers. Generation Z are now organized and mobilized to fight discrimination with the same passion that they are fighting climate change. You will not be able to compete for their skills or custom if you fall short.

Finally, at the end of this year of chaos and crisis we must also add the business complications of Brexit.

Brexit

At the time of writing in October 2020, the British government is advising business to prepare for Brexit at the end of the year. But as yet no deal has been struck with the EU, meaning that no business leader knows what specifically to prepare for. Uncertainty kills commerce and so leaders are game planning alternative scenarios for their companies, but they don't have a helicopter view of the big picture and the wider impact on the economy. Will there be food shortages and supply chain delays? Will there be tariffs that could become a block to business? Will firms in the supply chain go bust, leading to production stoppages, and as companies increase redundancies, will consumer confidence be hit?

Now more than ever before, leaders need diverse gender-balanced executive teams that can act swiftly, spot future consequences and opportunities, make robust decisions and adapt quickly to doing business in an unpredictable complicated landscape and uncharted territory.

A brain drain is already happening because of Brexit. The EU citizens that have stopped coming to work in the UK are not all baristas and hotel staff; many are engineers, software developers, managers, medics and nurses. These highly skilled people have the training, qualifications and skills that we so desperately need, and although some may still meet the criteria to be able to work in the UK, many are now choosing not to come to what is perceived as a hostile environment for them.

There is a glimmer of hope emerging, however, as a result of companies embracing remote working during the pandemic. Perhaps despite losing the freedom of movement as a result of leaving the EU, the freedom to work in other countries can still be maintained through digital means. UK employers could still access the skills of European citizens working in their home country, and European companies could employ British-based workers.

So it is essential to ensure that your business is an attractive proposition to anyone, wherever they are based, with the skills that you are looking for; and the talent pool includes a significant proportion of women of all ethnicities. You must not lose out to your competitors and let them optimize the potential of this resource instead of you. With the 'survival of the fittest' in mind, those businesses that are best adapted to this swiftly changing environment will thrive and survive.

Summary

When working in Ford of Europe in the early 2000s, my colleagues and I were given the book *Who Moved My Cheese?* by Dr Spencer Johnson. The European subsidiary company was facing such severe financial difficulties that we resorted to taking every other light bulb out in offices to save costs, and the book was sent from the US parent company to explain the attitude we needed to adopt. It's a simple story about mice in a maze having to adapt when one day their cheese supply disappeared. It's an analogy for the importance of rising to life's unexpected challenges through adaptability, flexibility and problem solving.

The burning platform of 2020 has well and truly moved our cheese. Many will be trying to find their cheese in the same place as before, and showing little ability to adapt to the new normal. However, some will have looked for a way to solve the problem with agility and speed, collaborating with and leading others with emotional intelligence. Such adaptability and agility is one of the core qualities of inclusive organizations, which are therefore better able to respond to existential threats. During this troubled period of almost unprecedented upheaval and change, as the shape of business shifts and transforms to adapt to legislation, lost markets and the changes to customer and employee behaviour, these human skills are more important than ever before.

Now is the time to embrace transformation. As outlined in the next chapter, to do this we must first eliminate the fear of positive discrimination.

4 Slaying the dragon of positive discrimination Dispelling myths and creating legends

It's now time to be realistic about the challenge that lies ahead, because we are up against myriad myths, rumours, supposed universal truths, stereotypes, false assumptions, wilful blindness and those who are perhaps well meaning but very ill-informed.

The dragon that must be slayed is the multi-headed monster that breathes the fiery words of 'positive discrimination'. It aggressively attacks any attempt to tackle inequities and create a level playing field for women or ethnic minorities. The angry dragon is unleashed to forcefully assert that actions to remove such discrimination will in fact lead to discrimination against white men. It is usually set free by the mediocre male rather than the talented man who is confident in his abilities to compete fairly. It is often drawn upon by those who deny the existence of inequity out of lack of awareness or prejudice. It is even used by women who mistake the removal of unfair advantage against them for special treatment or tokenism.

For the avoidance of any doubt, I strongly maintain that discrimination against anyone in any form is morally wrong. Token appointments on the basis of skin colour or gender hurt everyone, including the appointed, in the long run. Suggestions that solutions should be adopted to ensure white men are *disadvantaged* are unacceptable because two wrongs do not make a right. However, removing unfair advantage and giving fair treatment to all is a very different matter. It is essential that those who historically benefitted from an advantage learn that removing it is not the same as them being put at a disadvantage versus others, while also recognizing that when you're accustomed to privilege, equality could feel like oppression.

So to slay the dragon of positive discrimination we must name and dispel the damaging 'myths', and replace them in the company's collective memory with 'legends' that are facts and truths that make systemic unfair advantage transparent. We must then create the win-win solutions that benefit all parties.

There are many myths:

o   A male majority is a meritocracy

o   Targets drive positive discrimination

o   Get woke, go broke

o   She stole my job

I will now discuss each of these myths in turn, and suggest a new legend to replace them.

Myth: A male majority is a meritocracy

I have heard countless times 'I always hire the best person for the job; I don't care what their gender is.' Leaders often believe they preside over a meritocracy. They've risen to the top so they believe the system is fair and the best will succeed. But sometimes they change their minds when they get to the very top job. A female managing director of an engineering company once told me:

> I never believed that things needed to change for women to
> reach the top; I'd climbed the ladder without any help. But

when I became MD, I discovered the true level of incompetence
of some of my male direct reports, and I realized that they'd
been over-promoted to the detriment of the talented women I
knew, and the business.

An important protagonist in this myth is the 'Mediocre Male'. These men may be blocking top roles through default, lack of competition, or being in the right place at the right time, rather than merit. Every leader I speak to acknowledges that these men exist in their organizations, and that they probably wouldn't have been promoted had a wider talent pool been available. The mediocre male that has been promoted to a level beyond their competence is enshrined in Lawrence Peter's famous Peter Principle. There are of course mediocre females too; but they tend not to be over-promoted unless they are an ill-judged token female appointment. In fact, author Tom Schuller argues that women usually work one level below their competence, and has coined the term the Paula Principle to describe it.[1] It's likely the mediocre male will no longer be over-promoted when competing with a gender-balanced talent pool of top performers, and a reduction in management mediocrity will lead to an improvement in profits.

A report published in 2017 by the Black Business Awards identifies a 'paradox of meritocracy', whereby if a decision maker believes they operate in a meritocracy, the more they will show greater bias in favour of the already dominant group.[2]

A similar phenomenon is known as the 'Licensing Effect'. The more that leaders of a company convince themselves and pride themselves publicly on being a meritocracy, the more likely it is that individual managers will feel they have the licence to deviate from it and make a prejudiced hiring decision because they think there will be no overall impact from their actions because no one else is doing it. Unfortunately, they are usually not alone, and promotions based on merit become the exception rather than the rule.

The 2020 Parker Review suggests that the need to reassure that merit will not be compromised to achieve diversity is actually an indicator of inherent bias in the organization. This is because it implies that diverse boards would be difficult to create on merit, and that women and people of colour might not make the grade.³

A company where there is a significant imbalance in favour of males (or females for that matter) simply cannot be a true meritocracy. You may state that you hire on merit and that you don't hire on colour or gender, but if you are all white men you clearly are recruiting and promoting in a way that favours being white and male, albeit without realizing it. This is an uncomfortable truth for many senior executives who believe they rose to the top due to superior ability rather than because there were fewer hurdles to jump, or because talented women didn't want to or couldn't enter the race. There are norms that favour the hiring and progression of a certain profile of person, and in most industries it's the profile of the white man, some of whom will rise to at least middle management with varying levels of performance. It is not enough to say that women don't apply, or there aren't any women out there. If talented women are not applying, it's most likely due to the macho image or reputation of your company or sector.

The real issue isn't just bias; it's usually also ignorance and lack of awareness of the issues. The forces at play include the different behaviours between the sexes and how the organization's decision makers value one set of behaviours over the other. Women will tend to believe that their hard work will be seen and rewarded, and feel uncomfortable with self-promotion and networking. Men will tend to understand that visibility to the top team and positive impression management is critical, and who you know will often be more useful than what you know. If both apply for promotion, the recruiter's familiarity and knowledge of a person will often cloud whether they actually are the higher performer.

Also, an organization can place obstacles in front of women that many men can simply jog around. The requirement to relocate relies on there being a supportive spouse willing to sideline their career; the expectation to attend a long-term residential development programme often depends on the availability of 24-hour childcare; the obligation to work long hours in senior roles depends on the ability to source both domestic and childcare support. More men than women have this level of support from their life partner. In my career, I've often been disappointed to see just how many men would apply for relocations and even accept them without discussing it with their wives; they knew that it would be impossible for their wife not to comply after the fact without appearing to seriously undermine them or damage their career.

An organization that is gender balanced and diverse is much more likely to be a true meritocracy because nothing has stopped a very wide range of people succeeding. So we must replace the old myth of meritocracy with a new legend: *Merit-Based Inclusion Creates a True Meritocracy.* The best person actually did get the job, irrespective of their sex or race or family status. Barriers to progression that gave an advantage to one type of person over another have been removed. Leaders are inclusive and are comfortable to promote people who do not look or think like them. Successful heterogeneous diverse teams are evidence of an inclusive meritocracy.

Myth: Targets drive positive discrimination

As the founder of a campaign with a target in the title, I am forever being challenged on these grounds. I would put my opponents into two main camps. The first are people who have never run a business unit by setting and using objectives to monitor and stretch performance; they have only been on the receiving end of them and would prefer not to be held to account for performance. The second are usually male leaders who want to be seen as flying the flag for feminism, particularly to female customers and the outside world, but are also giving a paternalistic pat on the head to all the 'great girls' in their team, offering to mentor them on fitting in better and 'leaning in' to the existing culture. These performative allies don't want to commit to make the necessary changes to become an inclusive organization that would actually enable women and people of colour to get to the top without submitting to the current norms and becoming more like white men, and so won't sign up to a target they know they won't achieve.

Both types are true believers in the myth of meritocracy. They misinterpret a target as a quota, and make assumptions that to get to that number, unfair token female appointments will be made. This is a deeply sexist view, and is unfortunately held by both men and women. It is sexist because it wrongly assumes there are not enough high-performing women in the wider talent pool for a target to be met within a realistic time frame. Of course, there are; they are working elsewhere and you need to hire them. It is sexist because it refutes the existence of the extra barriers that women face when climbing the career ladder. It is also sexist because it assumes that women make a conscious free choice with regard to staying at a level below their competence, and it rejects the existence of systemic bias.

We must replace the myth that targets drive positive discrimination with the new legend that: *All Winners Set Targets, and Targets Drive Success*. Targets are an absolutely essential part of any plan that a leader wishes to implement successfully. Without a goal, there will be no incentive to improve, no ability to measure progress and no ability to benchmark. A leader who can't aim for a target and be held accountable for doing their best to meet it will not be a winner.

Myth: Get woke, go broke

This is a phrase commonly used on social media by keyboard warriors opposing action to get a gender-balanced and diverse workforce. The claim is that such 'liberal and woke' efforts will harm the company, because women are not discriminated against in the modern world and feminists are simply exploiting organizations. They ignore the contrary evidence that companies with more female and diverse leaders outperform their competitors by a significant margin. They claim the status quo gives the best results, because they think that changing it puts them at a disadvantage and that actions to address an imbalance are discriminatory against men and will end up with the appointment of lower-performing women. They focus on untrue messages about financial damage because they know that many people want to know the business case, and so they aim to obscure the truth and will invalidate the facts about the financial benefits.

In February 2020, Alex Smith, the Managing Director of VW Group UK, posted his thoughts on LinkedIn about a list of the top 50 movers and shakers in the motor industry, expressing disappointment that there were only three women on the list. A large volume of very positive responses agreed with his comments. However, a man working in a supplier company responded aggressively:

> So you want the judges to manipulate the results to achieve 50/50 gender parity in a field overwhelmingly of interest to men? Just so you can virtue signal about your hash tag Diversity nonsense? Get bent!

A female observer pointed out that the discrimination assumption was wrong. His response was again aggressive, wilfully ignored her point and denied the existence of inequity:

> Is that because those evil men are conspiring to keep women down because… patriarchy and misogyny? You can get bent as well. White, western women are the most privileged people on this Earth… bar none.

He went on to imply that instead of seeking equity, women are actually seeking an advantage over men. This is where we see the fear of losing his advantage revealed:

> Is it just another excuse for feminist activists to gain an advantage? I don't really blame opportunist grifters from insinuating themselves into organizations and turning a buck from this non-theistic religion that includes the gospel of Diversity & Inclusion. You go girl and ride that gravy train for all it is worth. The bean counters will eventually realize there's no money in it. Get woke, go broke!

This single example serves to underline the strength of feeling that some people have about their misplaced belief that gender-balance action leads to positive discrimination, how vocal they will be in expressing it in a public forum, and how ill-informed they are. I am often bewildered by the degree of hostility and vitriol shown towards me and other equality campaigners on social media, including threats of rape and violence.

The myth that gender balance leads to discrimination against men and is costly virtue signalling must be dispelled and replaced with the legend that: *Diverse Gender-Balanced Teams Are Equitable and More Profitable.* Selecting the best complementary mix of skilled people is a winning strategy.

Myth: She stole my job

Michael Kimmel is an American sociologist specializing in gender studies. He holds the position of Distinguished Professor of Sociology at Stony Brook University in New York and is the founder and editor of the academic journal *Men and Masculinities.* In his book, he recounts the tale of when he appeared on a TV show with the theme 'A Black Woman Stole My Job' opposite three angry white men who were convinced that they had been victims of reverse discrimination. They believed that they had lost a job possibility to a less qualified woman. They were only applicants for the role, not incumbents. Kimmel focused on the word 'my', and asked them what they meant by the job being theirs when they were each just one of many applicants. He pointed out that they seemed to feel entitled to the job, and that they felt the person who got it was really taking 'their' job. He asked by what right was it that they saw it as theirs; and suggested that it was through convention and a historical legacy of discrimination against women. The black woman in fact got 'the' job, not their job; it was a competitive process and it was never theirs for the taking, but they had assumed it would be. Kimmel asserts that when we have to compete equally for rewards that we used to receive simply by virtue of our race or sex, it feels like discrimination.[4]

The fact that the men refused to accept that a black woman could possibly have been better suited to the job than they were, and the belief that she must only have been appointed as a token diversity hire revealed either racism or sexism and likely both. This sense of entitlement to jobs and a self-belief that you must be better than a woman, combined with the disbelief that the competitive process was fair if they lost to a woman, fuels the claim that decisions are purposely being made in favour of women.

So the myth that a woman prevents a man from getting the job he believes he is entitled and best qualified for must be dispelled and replaced with: *Women Don't Steal Men's Jobs; They Earn Them.*

Summary

The dragon of positive discrimination must be slain, and the myths that surround it about meritocracies, targets and unfairness must be dispelled. The denial of the existence of sexism, racism and inequity can be just as dangerous a monster, and we will discuss how to overcome resistance to the adoption of inclusive norms in the next chapter.

5 Overcoming barriers and handling resistance Inspire, inform and reform

As mentioned in earlier chapters, unless you've already spent years laying the foundations for people in your organization to think inclusively, or you've recruited from younger and more open-minded talent pools, it's likely that you will face resistance to the change you are now implementing. The resistance is most likely to come from a small number of men who are accustomed to having a position of privilege and have enjoyed an unfair advantage. That means that they may view attempts to remove the unfair advantage they have as actually unfair to them. According to the author Michael Kimmel: 'Equality will feel uncomfortable for those who once benefited from inequality.'[1] It may also come from women who feel that they're being patronized or treated as if they're not as capable as men and so need special assistance. They think if they benefit from the changes, it will undermine their reputation for being able to compete without help.

Men and women must understand that the culture change will benefit all. It's about scouting for and putting together the best complementary talents to form a high-performing team. It's about acknowledging that the reason the team has not had gender parity or diversity historically is not that there aren't any capable women, but that organizations have been designed to fit around prejudices that are invisible, pervasive and endemic in the system. That leads to some people advancing and others being held back unfairly (sometimes by themselves) and we have not previously realized it.

As in any cultural change programme, it's necessary to 'thaw' the current norms and expectations and 'refreeze' them into the new inclusive shape of your business. To do this, you must inspire your team with motivating stories, identify objections and overcome them by informing them of the evidence, include your team in reforming your processes and policies so that they take ownership, and identify champions and change agents at all levels.

It is useful to develop an inspirational five-minute team talk that describes why you are making the changes and what the benefits will be. It's a great way to distil the key points into a motivating and powerful pitch, and will describe the norms that you will establish for your inclusive team. It's also important to have a set of anecdotes or stories to help explain some of the more complex issues and inform your colleagues of the facts.

To successfully build inclusive teams you must inspire and inform your people and reform your culture. You must:

o   Encourage openness and curiosity

o   Develop a nudge strategy

o   Create a safe space

o   Communicate that it's not a zero-sum game

o   Perfect a five-minute pitch

o   Share inclusion stories

Let's explore each of these tasks.

Encourage openness and curiosity

Fear of change is normal. It's important to get the support and buy-in of your colleagues in order to drive change. According to the previously mentioned Black Business Awards 2017 report, there is:

> ... a tendency to reject or over-scrutinize information that does not fit with our personal experiences, while on the other hand there is a failure to challenge information that does correspond with our beliefs. Lived experiences and statistics regarding 'the other' or 'the unknown' are often subject to a defensive reaction.[2]

Your team must be made aware of this risk of unbalanced processing. One of the new cultural norms needs to be to approach new, alternative ways of working and equitable and inclusive protocols with openness and curiosity rather than closed thinking.

Develop a nudge strategy

We can encourage people to support an inclusive culture by drawing upon nudge theory. Richard Thaler and Cass Sunstein's 2008 book brought nudge theory to prominence as a way of altering people's behaviour without explicitly forbidding other options or trying to alter their views. The theory suggests that most people are 'conditionally cooperative' in order to avoid being different to the norm.[3] The UK Behavioural Insights team in 2011 found that late payers of tax paid up when they were informed they were one of a small minority who hadn't paid. An earlier letter telling the recipients that nine out of ten paid on time didn't have as much impact as telling them they were one of the one in ten offenders and pointing out they were an outlier from the group. Generally, people want to run with the herd. People are more likely to adopt behaviour if they know that most others are already doing it. We sometimes refer to this as *herding behaviour*; the behaviour of the herd informs us as to what is normal, appropriate or beneficial to do. And we then do likewise. This suggests that, when requiring our team to adopt required behaviours, we can turn *descriptive* norms about what many people are doing into *prescriptive* norms just by telling people about them.

Of course, the herd doesn't always do the right thing. People do more bad things if they think that others are doing them as well, such as panic buying, leaving litter on beaches, or micro-aggressions and misogynistic comments. The keepers of the Arizona Petrified National Park made the mistake of telling visitors how many fossils were being stolen by people taking souvenirs. This actually increased the number of people doing it.

So you must avoid bombarding your team with information about how endemic sexism is. Instead, publicize the commitments to gender balance made by the growing number of inclusive leaders and share the progress many firms are making. You must make visible the women in key roles in both your organization and others to demonstrate that female leaders are not an anomaly. Focus on those in your team who are doing it right, so that others feel peer pressure to conform to that norm and 'name and fame' them.

Create a safe space

Business leaders who have instigated change in their companies will be well aware that it is often experienced as threatening, and so resistance is both understandable and normal. The Black Business Awards 2017 report points out the importance of creating a safe space for people to express their struggles with the new norms. They found that anxiety is often at the heart of group conflict, and that conversations about social identities are anxiety inducing, so they suggest that it is important to create psychologically safe spaces to accommodate those feeling vulnerable.

Everyone will be approaching this from a different starting point depending on family background, values, beliefs and social programming. You will probably never change their innate beliefs and nor should you make it your mission to do so. However, you should make it clear what the expected behaviour is, and that the company has values of dignity and respect. People should feel safe to express their concerns and if they feel threatened by the new norms, they should be listened to and reasoned with, and reassured that those who adopt inclusive practices have nothing to fear. Offer help and training if they feel they would benefit.

Communicate that it's not a zero-sum game

In economic theory, a zero-sum game is a situation where each participant's loss or gain is balanced by the losses and gains of other participants. The total sum of all gains and losses is zero. If one person wins, another one has to lose. Gender equality is not a zero-sum game. If a woman wins, it doesn't mean that a man needs to lose. If only one side wins, it creates a dent in the relationships and the culture will not be inclusive.

For this to work, you need to cultivate an abundance mindset in your team rather than a scarcity mindset. The scarcity mindset sees a limited availability of everything, so the person feels they have to get the most they can out of scarce resources. This person needs to have the last word to have won, be first in the queue, and may take credit for others' work to appear to be the best. They blame others for their failures or not getting a promotion because they think success was rightfully theirs.

An abundancy mindset sees that collaboration amongst people achieves more success for everyone and that defining everything as a competition that must be won means someone unnecessarily loses.

Those with a scarcity mindset who have been waiting for senior roles will not want new competition from diverse women. They may see their slice of the top management pie getting smaller. People who benefit from existing practices and norms may resist when their advantage disappears. The 'fixed pie' mentality is a known barrier to creative problem solving, effective decision making and teamwork because competition becomes focused internally within the company instead of externally. If people feel threatened by internal competition and new entrants, they will be less welcoming.

It's important to communicate that gender balance is not a zero-sum game; there doesn't need to be winners and losers. Everyone wins when the company is more successful, jobs are secure and rewards are high. If we all work together, we all win; but if we don't, we all lose. Business transformation and growth is a useful trigger because the pie itself gets bigger so there are more roles to fill. In an economic downturn, if the company is downsizing the conversation is harder because the pie could be shrinking for everyone.

Women's employment rates are higher in contexts where men are more confident in their own security and ability, have a more favourable view of competition from women as equals, and understand how a gender balance leads to better business performance – and even an improvement in their own performance as they 'up their game'.

Everyone must be fully aware that a key performance indicator in your organization is the building of inclusive teams so that as men become advocates for gender balance and allies of women, rather than seeing them as a threat, they will have personal career success because the business is more likely to succeed. To address the fixed pie mentality, introduce effective succession planning processes focused on the individual. This ensures the person has a career plan that is best for them and the business. It makes available multiple realistic progression opportunities rather than the person having a narrow (and possibly unrealistic) view of what their next step must be and competing aggressively for it.

Perfect a five-minute pitch

Here is an example of a compelling pep talk that sets the scene and explains to your team what change is needed.

We're transforming the business and building a winning team.
To beat the competition and achieve better business results, we

must be agile, adaptable and quick to respond to the wave of external events hitting us.

Women influence most purchases, yet our products are designed, engineered, produced and sold mainly by men. We must do better to understand and provide for our marketplace and our stakeholders. We are standing on a burning platform; we have a huge deficit of higher-level 21st-century skills, due to the acceleration of automation, the changes in customer profile and buying behaviour, and a growing need for the human skills of empathy, critical thinking, collaboration and ethical judgement. We need to tap into the underutilized female talent pool and cast the net much wider than ever before to find the most skilled people. Our competitors are already doing this so we must act fast so we are not left behind.

We need to think smarter, be efficient and effective, and use our collective company intelligence to be creative and innovative. We need a variety of different people to bring their different qualities and strengths to complement each other and make the sum greater than each individual part. This is diversity.

Evidence shows that gender-balanced diverse teams create better solutions, make better decisions and achieve better results; they outperform their peers by up to 25% in profit terms. Performance is greater when no one is excluded, when we are all confident to contribute different ideas, when we are all listened to as we give different perspectives, and when we are all valued for our efforts irrespective of our sex and ethnicity. This is inclusion.

Our team will show respect for each other and uphold fairness and equitable treatment. We will aim for gender parity over time and include diverse people of both sexes because it makes business sense, it will make us more successful, and because it is what society needs. It is not a zero-sum game, because everybody wins. To be a winning team we must change the game.

You get the picture. Now you must write your own authentic words and pitch it to your team.

Share inclusion stories

Storytelling is an effective way to help people better understand complex issues. Here are some useful facts and stories that you can use to inform your colleagues:

Women are not a minority

It is important not to subjugate female representation under the banner of a diversity initiative. To see it as existing within diversity is wrong because it takes the viewpoint that the 'non-diverse' person is the white man, and everyone else including all types of women are simply a deviation from that white male standard. Women are the majority of the population and arguably the biggest consumer market. There are more white women than there are white men. Diversity is therefore what we must seek within both the women and men (and people who adopt either gender) we employ. Although many seem to forget, diversity of course includes white people.

If we lose the focus on sex and gender as a starting point, it minimizes the importance of ending bias against more than half of the population, frames white women as a minority group, and diminishes the likelihood of recognizing additional barriers faced by women of colour through intersectionality. A black woman's barriers to progression are different to a black man's, and also very different to a white or Asian woman's. Don't assume that everyone who is not a white man will benefit from a standard programme of activities under a single diversity banner. There is a risk that although we may make great strides to address diversity, if we don't tackle gender-balance challenges, the majority of the diverse employees will still be men.

The winning team story

Your organization is a super-team of individual mini-teams and every member has to realize that they all need to give their best performance for the team to win. You must reassure your team that discrimination against anyone in any form is morally wrong, and that you will not adopt policies through which white men are *disadvantaged* relative to others. We do not create equitable conditions and help the injured player by kicking other players in the team and injuring everyone equally. We help the single injured player to overcome their disadvantage so they can contribute their skills and talent on the pitch. All must understand that the organization wins and beats the competition when diverse team members are included, are all match fit, are given an equitable chance to contribute and can play to their strengths and optimize their performance.

Equity versus equality
Many organizations mistake equality for equity. Both promote fairness, but equality treats everyone in the same manner regardless of need, whereas equity treats individuals differently according to their need. Proudly claiming that employees will have the same opportunities irrespective of gender or colour simply does not recognize the inequities that exist that prevent many of them accessing those opportunities. This fallacy of fairness exists in many companies.

A great way of illustrating this is the famous cartoon that depicts three people standing on small boxes to look over a wall at a sports match; one person is tall, one is average height, the other is small. The boxes are all the same size, so despite all standing on a box, only the tallest can see over the wall to watch the match. This represents equality; the boxes they stand on are equal, yet due to the height advantage of the tallest he is the only one that benefits. In the next cartoon the three are standing on different-sized boxes; the smallest person has the tallest box, the average height person has a middle-sized box, and the tallest person stands on the small box. This represents equity; they had a different box according to their need. All can now comfortably see over the wall. The tallest had an unfair advantage that was removed, but he is definitely not now disadvantaged because he still has a great view.

The levelling of the playing field did not take place at ground level; it happened at eye level.

As an employer, you can immediately see the benefit of having all three employees reaching the same high performance level rather than just one. Unfortunately, the tallest person will sometimes feel the ability to reach that level is a competitive advantage that he is entitled to, and resist actions that give the others a chance to overcome the disadvantage that is through no fault of their own. It suits him for you to only have a pool of one to choose from.

The difference between equity and equality is an important one. To create an inclusive organization, there must be a collective recognition that people need equitable rather than simply equal treatment in order to overcome unfair disadvantage.

Take a step forward
This is a game often used to illustrate social inequities, and here the focus is gender. It is a simple way of showing some of the invisible hurdles that women face. The leader lines up a group of men and women, and tells them they are in a race to the finishing line, but can only take a step forward if they can answer no to the questions. She then asks the following:

o   Have you had to leave an event earlier than colleagues so you could get home safely?

o   Have you had to laugh at an offensive comment or action in order to appease someone?

o   Have you ever been told to smile?

o   Have you had your input at a meeting repeated by a colleague who then gets the credit for the idea?

o   Have you been asked what your partner thinks about what you do for work?

o   Have people ever described you as emotional or hysterical when you were just angry?

o   Have you been asked how you manage to work and be a parent?

o   Have you been asked if your partner is 'babysitting' the children while you are at the event?

By the end of the questions, the person who answered 'no' to the most questions will have crossed the finishing line, and that person will be a man. Some women may have got quite far, but many would not have been able to step forward once.

The questions relate to how women are expected to be pleasers and appeasers, are expected to be primary carers, cause surprise if they don't conform to stereotypes and have to adapt their behaviour in order to stay safe. These factors hinder the progression of many women.

The game could be repeated with gender stereotypical attributes associated with caring that would show women in the lead and highlight the damaging effect this has on men's confidence and willingness to be a primary carer.

The littering story
Sometimes sexist and racist behaviour takes the form of micro-aggressions, which on the face of it seem relatively insignificant as individual instances, but accumulate over time to have a pernicious influence and create a toxic culture. The writer and consultant John Amaechi uses the analogy of littering to describe how each micro-aggression needs to be picked up, just as with each piece of litter. Otherwise, if no action is taken against littering, everyone starts to see it as acceptable behaviour and we all do it. No one feels it is their responsibility to pick up the litter. They all follow the norms of the herd. Then suddenly someone new comes into the workplace and all they can see is everyone wading through the rubbish and no one doing anything about it. All they can see is the everyday sexism; the comments about appearance, the offensive jokes, the ridiculing, the patronizing tone and the inappropriate touching or space invading.

It must be made clear to everyone that it's their responsibility not to say or do sexist things, and if they see anyone else doing it they must call it out before it becomes the norm. The litter must be immediately picked up. The victim should never have to be the one that does that.

Summary

To build an inclusive culture and be an inclusive leader you need to inspire others to embrace and support the benefits of diversity. You need to ensure they are fully informed of the issues, listen to their concerns and reassure them so that they feel invigorated rather than threatened by change. Also make sure you gain their commitment and support to participate in reforming the behaviours, policies and processes that shape the cultural norms in the organization. Creating a compelling change story, with illustrative anecdotes and an inspirational pitch, will help you to convince your team that now is the time to transform.

The next two chapters will reveal the different roles men and women can play to build a gender-balanced business.

6 What men can do: Sponsors, advocates, mentors and allies

It's impossible to build a winning gender-balanced business without including men. It won't happen unless men realize they are half of the gender equation and they need to do their bit to make sure that both they and the other half can thrive. Male leaders need to set a good example to other men and recognize inclusive behaviours while calling out incivility. Do not expect women to lead the gender-balance programmes; many are reluctant to do so for fear of being seen as doing it for personal gain. Women's networks will never achieve their goals if they are only talking to other each and the men in the positions of power can't hear them or don't want to listen to their suggestions.

The top team, currently predominantly white men, are in the positions of power and they must be allies of women and lead the change, while listening carefully to the needs of women and involving diverse women and men to ensure the actions will be successful. As Archbishop Desmond Tutu said: 'It is by standing up for the rights of girls and women that we truly measure up as men.'[1]

Leaders must look at their cultural norms and identify if any result in the exclusion of certain groups. For example, if a significant company social event is related to football, or in the evening or a weekend, it is likely to exclude many women. Choose something that is appealing to and accessible by all.

There are many ways that men can help to build gender-balanced teams:

o   Protect everyone, patronize no one

o   Be a sponsor

o   Be a mentor

o   Be an ally

o   Work for a female boss

o   Be an advocate

Let's examine each of these actions.

Protect everyone, patronize no one

Men need to ensure undermining behaviour is called out and hostile workplaces cultures are not tolerated. This is because we are still at a point where men will take more notice if men are calling it out than if women are, particularly if the men are more senior or held in high regard. Usually the balance of power works in favour of men (sexual harassment rarely happens to women who are more senior than the perpetrator). People must be protected from this abuse of power, and as we are still at the point where women tend to be in less powerful positions than men in most organizations, they may need more protection. BAME and gay men may also need protecting from abuse.

Professor Rosie Campbell of King's College London surveyed 272 senior women and 74 men. Women had more experience of incivility than men, with top female executives more likely to have experienced it than their male peers; 33% of these women said someone at work had made disrespectful or insulting remarks, compared to only 13% of men. Senior executives may have an unrealistic view of what happens lower down the management levels; senior respondents were more likely to perceive their current workplace climate as one that fosters inclusion than junior respondents. Leaders play a key role in signalling what behaviours are acceptable, and can nurture respectful behaviours by rewarding action they want to champion. They can also ensure workload allocation is appropriate to mitigate stress, which is a key trigger for workplace incivility.

A hostile environment endorsed by managers is a key reason why people leave the organization, yet it's unlikely it will be expressed in exit interviews due to a fear of retribution in references. The survey found that people who had experienced incivility from seniors often or many times were more likely to think about quitting their job and had lower job satisfaction. It's important to identify problems via workplace surveys and create plans of action to tackle incivility. Professor Campbell notes: 'Where there are hostile workplaces we can't simply ask women to lean in and try harder to reach leadership positions.'[2]

A hostile culture hurts everyone and so must be diagnosed and changed, and all employees must be protected from micro-aggressions, bullying and harassment. Women are more likely to be subjected to it in the early stage of their career so you must investigate if this is the reason junior women are leaving or not progressing. I will explore the effects of hostile environments on the retention of female employees further in Chapter 14.

In taking action, it is essential however that you don't patronize women. Women are not weak and helpless; they are capable of fighting their own battles and can at times be perpetrators of incivility as well as victims. It's important to discuss how best to avoid patronizing women with your female colleagues. Micro-aggressions shouldn't be framed as only ever being carried out by men to women. The norm must be to treat all others with dignity and respect, and that inappropriate comments and behaviour should be called out whoever the perpetrators and victims are.

Be a sponsor

A sponsor is a person with power, who is prepared to use it to help the sponsored person. They use their influence and networks to connect subordinates to high-profile assignments, people, pay increases and promotion. A sponsor is usually a senior leader whose opinion and judgement others respect. Women are usually over-mentored but under-sponsored compared to men, and so leaders must consciously ensure they are sponsoring both sexes. Formal sponsorship programmes to support the career progression of junior and middle-ranking staff can make this more of an expected norm in the organization and remove any suggestion of favouritism or nepotism. I have been struck when interviewing successful women or listening to their career stories that all of them had an influential senior sponsor who spotted their potential and encouraged them to seek promotions.

Be a mentor

Mentors support mentees through discussions about how to build skills, qualities and confidence for career advancement. The traditional mentoring relationship tends to involve individuals with years of experience in their field, who can guide an individual with less experience, helping to shape their future career goals and success. They can offer insights into the world of work and help to develop business confidence.

A mentoring programme that brings together the genders benefits both participants. A male mentor of a female mentee, or a female mentor of a male mentee can help to broaden the perspectives of both sides.

Formal mentoring programmes can be more effective than informal ones because the way a mentor or mentee choose each other informally could mean they gravitate to someone they already like or think will like them. Different and complementary experiences and insight are in fact more useful.

It's essential to take into account the different levels of comfort people have with building a mentoring relationship across the sexes. Men and women will be comfortable in same-sex mentoring meetings in informal surroundings, but that is not likely to be the case for a male–female mentoring relationship due to the unfortunate connotations with office romances or 'MeToo' type harassment. For that reason, mentoring discussions should happen in the workplace or at a distance through video calls, in usual work hours.

Don't be a mentor who tries to take credit for a woman's success. I've noticed when businesswomen post on social media that they've been promoted or achieved success, there is often a man from her past who posts a comment like 'Right from when I showed you how to do the job I've known you were destined for the top' or 'Those years of mentoring you paid off!' It implies she would not have achieved it without him. I don't think I've ever seen a man take credit for another man's success in this way.

Be an ally

Many men don't think that gender-balance or diversity issues are anything to do with them because they see them as women's issues. They often forget that they are the other half of the gender balance, and they are one of the types of diverse people (white people often mistakenly do not see themselves as represented within diversity). An ally recognizes that they have a role to play in reaching a gender balance and is supportive of women and wants to help ensure possible inequities are eradicated. Allies attend gender network meetings and understand that it is of benefit to them to understand the issues women face if they are to be an effective leader of inclusive teams. They adopt new practices to ensure women are not excluded.

Allies are important to 'nudge' other men into realizing that achieving a gender balance is everyone's job, and to be open to new ways of working. It's important to remember that many men have been brought up to view empathy with women as a sign of weakness. 'Laddish banter' promotes attitudes that see women as a strange species, subjects them to sexual objectification and often subordinates them. Feminists are depicted as jealous man haters who want to subordinate men. So when men publicly support gender balance, they're standing against this. This allyship with women takes confidence and courage due to the likely reactions from other less secure and well-informed men. This is why it's important that men at the top who others respect become advocates and praise other men for being male allies rather than leaving it to the women to do so.

Beware of the 'performative' allies though; these are the people who give the impression that they are supportive of equality simply as a tool to further their own career or reputation, rather than genuinely believing it to be the right thing for the business and taking action. As in the motto of the suffragette movement, an ally can be evaluated by their 'deeds not words'.

Work for a female boss

Many of the progressive male advocates I know have worked for a female leader during their career. They learned important leadership skills from that woman, which led to them rejecting the traditional stereotypical macho leadership style, and they have first-hand experience of high-performing women who they respect. Men need to be more accepting of women leaders, and this will happen when they become the norm not the exception. Ask to be mentored or sponsored by a woman if there is little chance in the short term of working for one.

Be an advocate

An advocate publicly supports, defends or speaks in favour of gender balance and inclusion. They not only take a leadership stance in their own organization and establish new cultural norms; they are also willing to express their beliefs in public forums and urge others to do the same. They play an essential role in creating positive peer pressure and use their positions of credibility and respect amongst male leaders to encourage them to see the benefits of gender-balanced businesses. As an advocate, you must also be a member of gender-balance networks to listen and learn and take action on the feedback and suggestions they make.

In an essay for *Fortune* magazine, Warren Buffett, Chairman and CEO, Berkshire Hathaway, proposed that women were the key to the US's future prosperity: 'Fellow males, get on-board. The closer that America comes to fully employing the talents of all its citizens, the greater its output of goods and services will be.'[3] This successful businessman, revered the world over by his peer group of predominantly male CEOs, took a significant step forward and proclaimed himself to be a male ally and advocate.

Many other business leaders have since followed and made public their commitment, and you should do the same.

Summary

Men are typically in the positions of power in business. They must become genuine allies of women and listen to their female colleagues to determine what is needed and how best to achieve it. Then they must use their power and influence to lead the charge and make the change, and encourage other men to do the same.

The next chapter will examine the role women can play to drive the change.

7 What women can do: Trailblazers, real models, growers and lifters

Women must also play their part in building inclusive teams. They must have the same high aspirations and expectations of success as male peers. They must fight gender stereotypes in both men and women and encourage all people to reach their potential and pursue the career that they will find fulfilling. It will help their own career plans if they build a personal brand that enables others to see quickly what their capabilities and talents are, and become well known in their field. They should also inspire others to progress, as Madeleine Albright, the first-ever female US Secretary of State, famously said: 'There is a special place in hell for women who don't help other women.'[1]

There are many ways women can help achieve the gender balance:

o   Build your personal brand

o   Get in the room and stay in it

o   Know your true worth

o   Go for it

o   Focus on your successes, not your flaws

o   Be a lifter

o   Be a grower

o   Be a 'real model'

o   Be a trailblazer

o   Be an advocate

We will now explore further each of these actions that women in business can take.

Build your personal brand

To be successful, you must build your own personal brand, and it's good to start early. People label others or stereotype them; it's easy to make assumptions and they may be false. If you don't build your own brand, then you will risk being given a brand that's not the one you want. People like to pigeonhole, in ways such as 'She's happy in her job; she isn't ambitious' or 'She's a great second-in-command'.

So take control of how others see you and what you want to be known for. What is important to you? What are your personal values? What are you passionate about? What makes you different? Why would anyone hire you? Be clear in what you stand for, stick to it and do it well. Think about what you would like to define you. Be proud of any deviations from the norm and how you stand out from the crowd because it gives you your unique point of differentiation over others. Once you've built your personal brand, it's essential that you make it very visible.

Get in the room and stay in it

I'm often told by women that they don't feel comfortable with networking. They think it means you have to talk about yourself a lot, or tell people how great you are. To them it seems superficial, with networkers only wanting to meet people who will be of use to them. They think it leads to favouritism or obligation.

A great networker actually doesn't say much about themselves at first; they ask lots of questions. They want to find out about other people in the room and look for a way of connecting with them, such as a similar experience or mutual friends. Once they've found that link, they build on it by telling the person about themselves in a way that will resonate with the listener.

Don't mistake networking for nepotism. It's actually important that people get to know you and can put a face to a name. If a group of senior executives have met you, it's easier for them to discuss your career potential than if you're just a name on paper. Having the ability to get on well with anybody no matter their background or where they work or what they do is also extremely useful. A diverse social and work network that transcends age, race and social background will help you to learn how to engage with people from all walks of life, to learn about and respect the differences and recognize what we have in common.

Women often lose out on 'getting in the room' because they choose not to attend company social events or conferences so that they can get their day job done and get home to the family. They think that by keeping their head down and hitting the numbers, the results will speak for themselves and they will be recognized and appreciated for their efforts. Sadly, this sometimes goes no further than the woman's line manager who takes the credit for her hard work, and is busy networking and explaining how he achieved it.

Try to get in the room, and stay in it. Don't spend the lunch breaks calling in to your team or family. Don't rush off before closing speeches to catch your train home. Make arrangements to ensure you can stay longer and talk to the people there because that will be the main benefit of having attended. Business does not happen by itself; it's the people and the relationships between them that make business happen.

Remember, it's not what you know, or even who you know, it's who knows you for what you can do. For them to know you, you've got to get out there and meet them.

Know your true worth

Winning businesses need women. The combination of men and women working together is far more powerful than men on their own, and both women and men benefit from the success it brings. So women are hugely valuable assets to the workplace.

Much research, including that of Caroline Hoxby of Stanford University, has found that both boys and girls benefit when there are more girls than boys in a class.[2] This is also true for executive training programmes. It is known as the 'girl effect' in education, and is why teachers are dismayed when they are given boy-heavy classes, and many independent boys schools introduce girls into their sixth forms. Both boys and girls underperform in boy-heavy environments – a lesson perhaps for the suboptimal performance of male-dominated workplaces versus their gender-balanced peers. Cognitively high-performing teams need women.

Unfortunately, women don't always realize their true worth and abilities. The validity of performance appraisals that use self-evaluations is therefore questionable because men have a tendency to give an inflated view of their own performance, and women have a tendency to underestimate it. If appraisals are then used to judge suitability for promotion and the information is taken at face value, it will appear that the women are not performing to the same standard as men. Although managers will often moderate the scores, they don't narrow the range sufficiently to overcome this phenomenon. It's essential therefore that organizations put guidelines and robust processes in place to eliminate the tendency towards modesty or performance exaggeration.

Women are more likely to do unpaid work in the home, which then impacts on their career and potential earnings. We hear women say: 'I stopped working because we realized that my earnings were just paying for the childcare.' It's a strange paradox because these couples will have pooled their financial resources, yet for this instance they are splitting apart again who earns what. The implication is that the couple don't view it as a financial contribution from both parties to care for their child. Why doesn't the man's salary also take the hit? Why is it that they don't see that they could both work part-time rather than pay for childcare? The woman has downgraded herself from an independent salary earner to be a financially dependent unpaid homeworker with an insecure future, potentially depriving another more qualified person from working as a professional child carer. The reason this is a socially acceptable thing to do is that women are often willing to be unpaid for their labour (and any mum of young children will testify that it certainly is hard labour) and men definitely are not. Men are more likely to have been raised to measure their worth and level of success in terms of their earnings and material possessions.

However, women must only do their fair share of unpaid work and select partners based on their willingness to do half of it. They must make sure that they don't sell themselves short.

Go for it

There is a commonly held belief that women lack confidence. This isn't actually true; it's just that relative to most men they appear less confident. Women don't lack it, but many men have an over-abundance. Many men openly express a high opinion of themselves whereas many women tend to avoid blowing their own trumpet. This probably results from it being socially acceptable for men to hold themselves in high regard while women are expected to be more modest and are disliked if they show high levels of confidence. A meta-analysis examining perceptions of leadership effectiveness across nearly 100 independent samples undertaken by Brad Barber and Terrance Odean in 2001 found that men perceived themselves as being significantly more effective than women did, when in fact they were rated by others as significantly less effective.[3] Women can also overestimate barriers and the level of performance required to succeed in a task, and so underestimate their ability to achieve success. Such identification of the potential pitfalls, whether real or imagined, leads to women holding back in order to avoid failure, where men (who don't spend time looking and so may be blissfully unaware of the challenges ahead) step forward.

Hewlett Packard's research found that their female employees only applied for promotions when they felt they met the criteria 100%, whereas men would apply when they met 60%.[4] IBM found that when they advertised for a Head of China Operations with the requirement to be fluent in Mandarin, no women applied but six men did. The women didn't apply because despite speaking Mandarin they were not fluent. None of the men could speak Mandarin at all. This doesn't show evidence of a lack of confidence amongst women; they simply followed the criteria. It shows an over-confidence and a disregard for the criteria by the men. It becomes a significant gender inequality problem for the company if ignoring the criteria is deemed acceptable by the recruiter and the man is hired anyway.

The key message to women then is stop overestimating the likely difficulties jobs may have, believe in your own ability to perform well, and go for it. You have nothing to lose and everything to gain. Try not to leave an organization until you have reached the first level of management. This is the most important rung to reach as swiftly as possible in order to progress.

Focus on your successes, not your flaws

Women are raised to be aware of dangers and to be risk averse. A heightened fear of failure could also be a manifestation of perfectionism. The recent global Programme for International Student Assessment (PISA) study of teenagers found that girls in the UK have one of the highest fears of failure of pupils anywhere in the world.[5]

To tackle this, focus on your successes not your flaws. It is important to play to your strengths and look at what you do well and be proud of that. I have spent many years training and coaching people. The traditional approach is to identify your strengths and weaknesses, and focus on correcting your weaknesses. I firmly believe that this is wrong, and you should actually focus on and build even further your strengths. You develop your expertise and become the best in the field. You really don't need to be good at everything, but you definitely do need to be good at something. Find what that is and excel in it. Accept that we all have flaws; that's what makes us interesting humans.

Be a lifter

Robert Ingersoll, the nineteenth-century American orator, is credited with saying 'We rise by lifting others.' It's essential that men and women lift others as they rise up through the ranks of the organization. You can help your business to get a better gender balance by ensuring that when you move up, you look back and extend a helping hand to ensure other women are ready and waiting to follow you.

Women's networks play an important part in supporting women and creating a forum for women to inspire other women to progress and lift others as they rise. Such networks must be inclusive for all ethnicities. Women must work together to understand how they can help each other to overcome their different barriers and also identify those that they all have in common.

To be a true lifter, it is a great idea to be a sponsor, coach or a mentor because it will help not only the mentee but also the organization and it will give you deeper insight and extra skills.

Be a grower

Not all women have the ability to reach senior roles, or indeed want to climb up the career ladder. There are many women who stay in the lower-level roles and help to set other women on their way by nurturing them, teaching and helping them to grow into accomplished high performers. Every successful woman is able to look back and remember their first female supervisor that taught them the ropes, or the secretary who always gave her a slot in the CEO's diary, or the group of older women who took her under their wing and created a firewall from the sexist comments of male colleagues. These women spot potential in young new starters, help nurture it, push them onto the first rung of the ladder and then turn around and do it all again for the next one. They're the unsung heroines of the organization because they play such a valuable role in equipping their young female colleagues with the skills to perform well and thrive. They're the springboard to success, without which many women would leave the company in their first few years. If you're one of these women, you should be proud of your contribution. If you know one, you should ensure they're praised and recognized for the important role they play.

Be a 'real model'

This is a hugely powerful way to help other women. We know how important it is for people to be able to see role models to emulate and admire. Seeing a woman in a non-gender stereotypical role reassures other women that it is possible and that they could do it: 'If you can see it, you can be it.' I prefer to use the term 'real model' because role model has connotations of perfection, and the woman doesn't need to be a perfect example or super-woman: they're just real, normal and good at their jobs. If a woman can relate to other women who have made it up the career ladder, they can be confident that they too could make it that far.

Women must not shy away from being 'real models' for fear of standing out and being more visible; that's exactly what is needed to help other women to progress. It's beneficial to you because it will get you known.

Be a trailblazer

But what if a woman hasn't done the job yet? Someone has to go first; why not you? We need women to aim for jobs even though no woman has been appointed in the role before. Amazingly, there are still many roles in business and other walks of life that have never been filled by a woman.

Katharine Meyer Graham became the first female CEO of a Fortune 500 company in 1972, as the Chief Executive Officer of the Washington Post Company. She was at the helm of the *Post* during the pivotal Watergate scandal. She was Chair from 1973 to 1991. Dame Marjorie Scardino became the first female Chief Executive of a FTSE 100 company when she was appointed CEO of Pearson in 1997. During her time there, Pearson's profits tripled, to a record £942m. In 2002, Baroness Sarah Hogg, Viscountess Hailsham, became the first woman to chair a FTSE 100 company when she took over the Chair role at 3i.

All of these women were trailblazers in their field and proved to be top performers. They led the way for many more businesswomen to follow their footsteps into top roles. We need many more women to do the same until no summit remains that has not yet been scaled by a woman. Then we need lots of female fast followers hot on their trail so that we avoid 'one and done'.

Be an advocate

Many senior women feel uncomfortable advocating for gender balance, particularly if they are the only woman in the top team and the only one championing the cause. They are concerned that it will paint them as a radical feminist looking to benefit or, even worse, a token hire appointed on a gender ticket. I admit that I was once that woman. However, it is time to look beyond that. Women leaders who are advocates for gender balance are an inspiration to their male and female colleagues and help to inform and motivate them to improve the culture and performance of the business.

Summary

Some women are at the top of businesses and therefore have the power to lead, influence and implement the change, being true advocates for gender balance, and lifting others. Others must be members of the grassroots movement, pushing themselves or others upwards on the career ladder. We are raised listening to fairy tales and folklore that paint women as the people who, in times of crisis, will be rescued by a man. Don't fall into the trap of asking a man to be your mentor and sponsor, and then hope that he will hack a path through the corporate jungle for you to glide through effortlessly. It's your responsibility to take advantage of any opportunity to progress, and you must be the hero in your own life story.

Men and women have different but complementary roles to play in building gender-balanced businesses. Most importantly, they must work together and collaborate to create winning diverse teams; it is not something that either sex can or should do alone.

Working together to create better life and career outcomes for both women and men will have a profoundly positive impact on society and could help you to find your own purpose and reason for being. We will explore this in the next chapter.

8 Find your purpose and reason for being: The wider impact on the world

In the previous chapters, I have outlined how important it is to have a gender-balanced diverse organization for your company to be successful, creating equilibrium in an ecosystem of different types of people that work together to achieve the firm's goals.

In order to reach personal fulfilment, however, you must aim for more than simply a successful business. This concept of balance and being part of a wider ecosystem should stretch beyond the organization and into your own life as an inclusive leader, and is beautifully articulated in the Japanese philosophy of Ikigai. Having worked closely with Japanese companies and visited Tokyo and Kyoto, I have always admired the Japanese skill of taking pride in perfecting even the smallest of tasks, and distilling complex and detailed concepts into a simple construct that is easy to communicate and understand; Ikigai is the perfect example.

Ikigai (pronounced 'eye-ka-guy') is your reason for getting out of bed every morning. It is your life's purpose. It helps you to live a life of intention and consequence and makes you happy. It is your 'raison d'etre'. It is not about making money, or having grand designs on changing the world. It is simply about living your life with meaning and purpose, finding joy in small things, being in harmony with people and the environment, being comfortable with who you are and living in the present.

However, in 2014 the blogger Marc Winn used the Purpose Venn Diagram to put his own interpretation on how a life lived with purpose achieves Ikigai.[1]

This interpretation suggests that you can find your Ikigai, or reason for being, in our modern western world if you have the right balance between vocation, profession, passion and mission. It has resonated with many thousands of people as a way of explaining how to achieve fulfilment, and recommends that you:

Do what you love to do

Do what you are good at

Do what you will get paid for, and

Do what the world needs

Each of these actions is represented as overlapping circles in the form of a Venn diagram. The area of overlap between doing what you love and are also good at is your *passion*. The overlap between what you are good at and paid for is your *profession*. The overlap between what you are paid for and what the world needs is your *vocation*, and the overlap between what the world needs and what you love to do is your *mission*.

Your Ikigai, your 'raison d'etre', is then found in the very centre, at the intersection where your passion, mission, vocation and profession converge.

I believe that this combination of the purpose diagram and the concept of Ikigai is a powerful one. It reminds us that wealth and success doesn't lead to happiness unless we are in harmony with what is good for society. Yet also we can't pursue what we love and are good at if it doesn't pay enough to put food on the table and a roof over our heads.

Figure 8.1: Ikigai Venn diagram.

Winn, Marc. What's Your Ikigai? The View Inside Me, 14 May 2014,
http://theviewinside.me/what-is-your-ikigai/

You're no doubt at or near the top of your profession and so
are likely to be well paid, and you got there probably because
you are passionate about what you do and are good at it. But
money on its own doesn't lead to fulfilment. You strive to
have enough, and perhaps even more than you need, but you
still don't feel fulfilled unless affluence is balanced with other
things. You will never stop driving to earn more and more
money unless you realize that on its own, it won't bring you
the self-actualization you crave. Your business is successful
because it is providing something that the world needs; thus
your vocation is achieved. But what is your mission? To feel
truly fulfilled, you must identify what you love to do and what
the world needs, so you must define and implement your
mission. This is not what you are paid for in your job. This
is what you will personally do for society because you feel so
strongly about it.

Marc Benioff, CEO and founder of Salesforce, notes:

> On the day we signed the incorporation papers, I knew
> that the measure of my success as a CEO — and in truth,
> as a person — would be the extent to which every future

employee found meaning in his or her work. By incorporating volunteerism and giving back at the start, we could build a culture with meaning.

He adds: 'So I decided that no matter how much Salesforce grew, it would donate 1% of its product, 1% of its equity and 1% of its employees' time to help non-profits and charities.'[2] This is what Benioff does to help society.

I'm introducing you to the purpose diagram because it's important for you to be aware that by being an inclusive leader, advocating for gender balance and diversity, and creating an environment in which women will thrive in order to get business success, you're also doing just what society needs. You may be able to reach your own Ikigai through your journey to a gender-balanced organization, because of the following:

o   You will inspire the next generation
o   More women will fulfil their career potential
o   More men will fulfil their carer potential
o   More people will be treated equitably and with dignity

You will inspire the next generation

Implementing outreach programmes to help youngsters in schools to overcome gender stereotypes will have a hugely positive impact on their future lives if they're free from the shackles of restrictive gender norms. You can help them to aspire to great things by inspiring them to gain higher academic or vocational qualifications, personal and social skills and an inclusive mindset. You and your employees could be brilliant 'real models' to them, so they see that someone like them could become as successful as someone like you.

Research by the charity Education and Employers in 2012 found that youngsters given four meaningful encounters with an employer during secondary school were 86% less likely to end up as a NEET (not in education, employment or training) and had 22% higher earnings than their peers.[3] In a later 2019 study, they found that participation in career talks with volunteers from the world of work could completely change the attitudes of 14 to 16-year-old pupils to their education. It can influence their future plans and subject choices, motivate them to study harder and support an improvement in academic attainment, even when taking place only a few months before their exams. Those predicted borderline passes for English GCSE increased their revision by 32% as a result of meeting employers. One in 25 students actually achieved a higher grade than predicted as a result of the extra effort. Lower achievers and less engaged learners responded best to the intervention.[4]

Planning a wide-ranging programme of school engagement activities for you and your employees to participate in will undoubtedly transform the lives of many of the youngsters you meet. We can all identify a person who inspired us in our formative years, and helped us to choose a career or lifestyle or adopt a set of personal values. Be that person for one of the youngsters of today.

More women will fulfil their career potential

By recruiting, promoting and retaining more women in your organization, you will be helping hundreds and maybe thousands of women to prove their abilities and value, reach their career potential and fulfil their ambitions. The actions you put in place to eliminate discrimination and remove barriers to progression will have a lasting positive effect on the lives of those women and their families. Each woman that rises through the ranks will be in turn a positive 'real model' to other women, and can lift others as she rises. Their sons and daughters will see them as career women and providers in the same way as their fathers. Over time, we may see girls aspiring to be engineers and top business leaders in the same numbers as boys, as it becomes normal to see women in those roles. Your daughter will benefit hugely from societal changes that ensure women can access as many opportunities as men and achieve economic parity and financial independence.

McKinsey & Company claim in their 2017 report that in the UK, a woman starts her life close to parity with men, but as she grows up the gap gets bigger due to the lack of political representation, the pay gap, the unpaid care burden and vastly disproportionate levels of violence against women. They estimated that a 6.8% increase in UK GDP (£150 billion) could come from getting more women in the workforce, more women working in productive sectors and women working on average 30 minutes more per day through being able to access flexible or agile working. It not only makes business sense to have more women in the workforce; it also improves the financial independence and status in society of women, and increases the productivity of the nation.[5]

More men will fulfil their carer potential

In 1967, the anthropologist Margaret Mead said: 'Every time we liberate a woman, we liberate a man.'[6]

I firmly believe that this is true. Introducing paid shared parental leave and increased paid paternal leave will enable more men to develop that all-important bond with their baby. It is unfair that many companies don't allow their male employees to care for their babies in the same way that their female employees can without severe financial penalties. There is growing evidence of the existence of paternal postnatal depression, sometimes as a result of a lack of antenatal information and preparation for childbirth and care. Difficulties managing new childcare responsibilities and emotionally supporting their partners, combined with a speedy return to work, can be overwhelming.

By adopting contemporary working practices such as flexible, agile and remote working and making them free of gendered associations, you will be liberating men to spend more time with their families.

According to Professor Eirini Flouri of University College London in her 2005 book, fathers play a crucial role in child development and subsequent adult status and behaviour. Key studies of fathers around the world have found that fathers' involvement with their children and their learning is linked with positive educational outcomes.[7]

A group of academics, Karin Grossmann, Klaus Grossmann, Elisabeth Fremmer-Bombik, Heinz Kindler, Hermann Scheuerer-Englisch and Peter Zimmerman, discovered from a study over 16 years that fathers' sensitivity in play when their child was aged two predicted the child's security at age ten, and significantly predicted the child's adjustment and self-worth at age 16.[8] Earlier research by Paul Amato of the University of Nebraska has indicated that the closer children are to their father, the happier, more satisfied and less distressed they are.[9]

Better mental health outcomes for fathers and better educational and emotional outcomes for children as a result of quality time spent together are without doubt hugely beneficial to society.

More people will be treated equitably and with dignity

By adopting an unequivocal anti-sexist, anti-racist and anti-homophobia stance, you will be sending a clear signal to your employees about what values and norms are acceptable not only in your organization but also in wider society. Make sure that people know where you stand: rather than being 'not sexist', you are fully anti-sexist and can be someone who makes other people want to be anti-sexist too. If you eliminate harassment and hostility towards women, people of colour and members of the LGBT+ community in your company, you will be relieving the suffering of a large proportion of your workforce. This will undoubtedly have a positive knock-on effect on their families and the local communities of your employees.

Generation Z is the first generation to see young white western men and women rejecting racism, sexism and homophobia on a scale never seen before. They want to live in a world where bigotry and intolerance are seen as norms of the past, not the present or future. They will be your employees, and by building an inclusive culture you will help them to create a society where people are treated equitably and with dignity irrespective of the colour of their skin, gender or sexuality.

Summary

I believe that you will find your purpose in life by matching what you love to do with what the world actually needs. By ensuring you are helping your community to thrive, helping youngsters to get a good start in life and helping to ensure that no person is treated badly because of their sex or skin colour. By paying a fair wage, creating a working environment that people feel happy in, reducing stress and factors that damage mental health. By helping people of both sexes to access opportunities that they could not before, and creating an environment in which they can thrive and reach their full potential. By ensuring your business is helping not harming the world, and nurturing not damaging society.

As you find your reason for being, you should pass on the philosophy to your teams to help them to enjoy their work and feel balanced and fulfilled by also helping others. I have observed that the more employees get involved in business activities that are for the good of humanity, the more they seem fulfilled.

Your life's purpose will help you to leave a lasting legacy because you are personally doing what society needs.

The following chapters outline a simple route map to building a winning gender-balanced business in the form of Six Steps to Success. I hope that you will also find your Ikigai as you go on the journey.

Part 2 The Six Steps to Success

9 Step 1: Know your data – Be accountable for progress

Before you set off on your journey to achieve a gender-balanced business, you must know your starting point. It's amazing how many companies spend money on diversity projects without knowing the actual level of gender inequality and diversity in their organizations. You must then create a plan to ensure you reach your goals, in full knowledge that what doesn't get measured can't be fixed.

In order to find out if, where and why there is imbalance in your organization, it's important to ensure you collect accurate people analytics data disaggregated by gender. You may wish to enable employees to identify themselves with additional gender categories to the binary male and female that is associated with each sex.

In order to understand how diverse your workforce is, you must also disaggregate it at least by ethnicity, bearing in mind that information about other types of diversity may be harder to gather until you have built a culture of trust. Always explain to employees that the data is confidential, why it's needed, and if necessary give them the option of 'prefer not to say'. The degree to which that option is used would be an indicator of the current level of trust.

The steps to take when creating your action plan are:

o   Collect female representation data

o   Set goals – Three is a magic number

o   Monitor parental leave, promotions, moves and turnover

o   Investigate reasons for gender imbalance

o   Identify priorities for going fast first

o   Hold senior management to account

o   Invest in future profitability

Collect female representation data

The first action is to collect the gender and ethnicity data for all current roles. This will enable you to identify if you have gender segregation by job role, management level and function, and also pockets of gender balance in certain work teams and significant imbalance in others. The UK population is 51% female, and even if we adjust this to take into account only the working population, we find only a slight change to 52% male and 48% female. So a workforce that has less than an approximate balance between the sexes has an underrepresentation of one of them.

In order to tap into the superior results that come from the inclusion of diverse people, your quest to recruit more women to achieve a gender balance must not end up with solely white women. There are 18 ethnic groups used in official classifications of ethnicity, which are then grouped into five primary groups. There are very important regional population differences that need to be taken into account. In London, the proportion of people self identifying as White British in the 2011 census was 44.9% but in the North East it was 93.6%. A London-based organization will have a much more diverse population to select from than other areas.

It's essential to know the levels of representation in your different recruitment markets. For example, graduate recruits selected from a UK-wide pool could be assessed against the

UK-wide ethnicity population levels whereas apprentices should probably reflect local mixes.

Although in UK organizations we have become accustomed to grouping all people who are not in the white category into one classification – Black Asian and Minority Ethnic (BAME), it is essential to avoid falling into the trap of not monitoring them as separate ethnic groups. Each group will bring different perspectives and face different challenges in terms of recruitment and progression.

The female representation data you must have at your fingertips has to cover all roles across the business. It is helpful to group it into the four pay quartiles used in the annual gender pay gap report rather than by simple management levels because then you can compare them with other companies. From 2017, any organization that has 250 or more employees must publish and report specific figures about their gender pay gap.

The gender pay gap is the difference between the average earnings of men and women, expressed relative to men's earnings. It is a measure across all jobs in the UK, not of the difference in pay between men and women for doing the same job. The median gender pay gap amongst all (including part-time) employees was 17.3% in 2019, and for full-time employees only, the gap was smaller at 8.9%.[1] The UK pay gap data serves as a useful benchmark for individual companies wishing to achieve a gender balance because a smaller gap indicates positive progress in terms of employing equal numbers of men and women in particular roles and levels in the organization.

Assuming you are not acting illegally by paying men and women differently for the same job, your pay quartiles will largely reflect the gender split in your management levels and those roles deemed to be of higher value to the business. It's common currently to see more women in lower pay quartiles and fewer women in the higher pay quartiles, and this imbalance must be addressed.

You should then analyse the data for the 'strategic apex' of the company. This includes the board, the executive committee and their direct reports. These are the leadership roles that are so critical to ensure an inclusive culture is driven from the top and optimal decision making takes place. You can benchmark this data against the FTSE 350 companies who submit data annually to the Hampton-Alexander Report. Also analyse the rate of appointment to these roles, and specifically which roles the women are filling; the business will reap more benefits of effective decision making if they are in critical jobs running operations (usually those with profit and loss responsibility) rather than in advisory roles with lower status.

Set goals – Three is a magic number

Now that you know where you are in terms of diverse female representation, you must set your long-term goal to achieve a better gender balance, and break it into smaller achievable steps in the short and middle term. You may wish to set goals for the levels of representation of all ethnicities, relating to local or national populations, but as a minimum you should define your target as 'all women' or 'diverse women' so that it is explicitly stated that your aim is that the group should not be homogenous.

As discussed in earlier chapters, there is evidence that a higher female representation at the top of the company leads to superior performance relative to less inclusive peers. It is essential therefore to include a gender-balance target in the top teams.

Organizations pondering how to best create teams should focus on achieving a 'critical mass'. Professor Rosabeth Moss Kanter of Harvard Business School proposed that relative numbers of socially and culturally different members of a group were critical in shaping the interactions and dynamics in group life. She observed that equal representation was not required to change experiences and team performance, and that 'one-third in relative terms and at least three in absolute numbers enables group dynamics to achieve the positive benefit of diversity'.[2]

As per the references to the sacred power of the number in many ancient cultures and texts, it would indeed seem that 'three is the magic number'. Your target therefore should be a minimum of a third representation of diverse women in the short to medium term to change the cultural performance, which will set the momentum going to achieve a longer-term goal of parity. This will be most successfully achieved through ensuring women are never in a minority of less than three in any group, and through the appointment of diverse female (and male) leaders in proportion with their representation in the wider community and your customer base. The 2017 Parker Review recommendations included that each FTSE 100 board should have at least one director of colour by 2021; and each FTSE 250 board should have at least one director of colour by 2024. This person could, of course, be a woman.[3]

In order to achieve higher levels of female representation at the top of the company, your short-term goal must be to achieve a better gender balance through the promotional pipeline, so you must identify a target for female representation in each of the pay quartiles. Aim for 50% in the lower quartiles to create a female talent pipeline, and at least 30% in the upper quartiles in the short term but parity over the longer term to ensure there will be a balanced pool from which to recruit the future leaders. High but achievable goals can be powerful nudges.

Monitor parental leave, promotions, moves and turnover

The level of uptake of paternity leave or shared parental leave is a useful indicator of the attitudes to gender stereotypes in your organization. If your policy is fair but take-up by men is low, you know that you have a pervading culture that views men who care for their children negatively. If your policy inflicts a financial penalty on men, then you are actually inadvertently causing an additional career barrier for women who lose out when male peers are not equally absent from the workplace. You must take action to ensure men take their full entitlement and ensure that your leave policy is fair to parents of both sexes. We will examine the importance of maternity, paternity and shared parental leave and their role in employee retention in further detail in Chapter 14.

Analyse the promotion rates of men and women and identify if and why you're not promoting proportionately. Also review lateral moves, demotions, foreign assignments, relocations and external hires by gender. Refuse to accept all-male shortlists from headhunters, and business leaders of national subsidiaries may need to push back if candidate lists being put forward to them for foreign assignments are not gender balanced.

It's important to analyse turnover and returner rates by gender; often there is balance in those leaving, but returners or new senior hires are men. If, however, more women than men are leaving, there is a reason why women are not thriving in those roles.

Investigate reasons for gender imbalance

Armed with your starting point, your people analytics and your end goals, you must examine the reasons why there is a gender imbalance in some or all of your organization, and create a plan to address it.

Investigate why roles are not currently (or have never been) filled by women. Is there a problem with hiring criteria (e.g. experience required, job design) or are there high attrition rates amongst women or stagnancy amongst men blocking the role? Review this information in order to understand the problem first. Avoid 'solutioneering', that is, assuming that the problem is because you don't have a particular solution in place (e.g. a mentoring scheme), rather than identifying the root problem and addressing it with a number of possible solutions.

> PwC thought they had a problem with women leaving and they needed to fix this by driving diversity programmes focused on the retention of women and particularly on support for new mothers. However, when they analysed the data they found that more women leave than men at the most junior grades only, and at this point in their lives very few of these women are at the stage of starting a family. At all other grades, more men actually leave than women. But they were mainly replacing both male and female leavers with male experienced hires.

In response to this insight, they have switched from a strategy focused mainly on retaining female talent to an approach today under which they have identified recruiting diverse experienced women as the solution.

Use the '5 Whys' Kanbanize problem-solving technique developed by Sakichi Toyoda, the founder of Toyota, to get to the root answer.[4] Start with your priority question, e.g. Why are there fewer women in middle management than in junior roles? Having identified the reasons, such as attrition of junior women, or fewer women going for promotion, or fewer women securing promotions, you again need to ask why that is the case. Carry on until you have asked why five times, and that will take you to the root cause.

Identify priorities for going fast first

As well as examining your people analytics data, you should read scientific findings from research and seek professional expertise from HR and D&I practitioners both inside and external to the company. The concerns and experience of stakeholders such as employee networks, line managers, executive sponsors, customers and clients will also help you to identify priorities.

After doing this, target specifically where to appoint more women. As you build your gender-balance credentials, note that it is better to address gender balance with a high proportion of women in just a few groups rather than put a single woman alone in many groups. In small group contexts, women and disadvantaged groups are more likely to be able to contribute more, because the degree of their representation is bigger and the competitive context is smaller. Look for small teams on the pathway to senior roles and implement gender balance in them first. It's important to achieve a critical mass of women in key groups, so I would suggest there is value in achieving at least 30% or more female representation in a few small teams where the role is a known stepping stone to promotion. This is preferable to spreading the women equally across the business where they will remain an insignificant and potentially ignored minority in each group. In a currently male-heavy environment, not everyone can be in a diverse team without turning some people into token group members.

It's also important to play to your strengths in the very short term. Your people analytics investigations will have identified where you already have women and inclusive leaders. Recruit more women to join them. Create a route to the top in the units where the culture has already begun to recalibrate, and use them as examples of best practice and evidence of performance.

Hold senior management to account

Senior leadership can delegate responsibility for taking action to build gender-balanced diverse teams, but not accountability. It's imperative to monitor the data at CEO level within your board's business management dashboard, and cascade the diversity goals via the management team's objectives using both short and longer-term key performance indicators (KPIs). You must hold senior employees to account for progress as you would for other performance objectives; through performance appraisals and bonus awards, rewarding and celebrating successes that indicate they are building high-performing inclusive teams. Try different solutions to see what works; and put in place policies to nudge behaviour towards more equality. Supporting equality in the workplace is the responsibility of all leaders and managers and shouldn't be something they can opt out of.

Invest in future profitability

When you have identified the size of the task that lies before you, it's necessary to allocate a realistic budget to achieve it within the desired timescale, reassured by the knowledge that it's an investment in the future profitability of the business.

It's essential to track the return on the investment, such as the higher calibre of applicants resulting from the additional cost of hiring a specialist recruitment agency, or increased female promotions as a result of investing in a coaching programme for women. It's also important to track improvements in overall business performance as the gender balance improves over time.

Investing in generous parental leave policies for both sexes will reap greater returns than it may first appear; it will significantly help to break negative gender stereotypes and help to close the gender pay gap.

Remember to avoid solutioneering or you may risk wasting money on actions that don't have any positive impact.

Here are case studies of two companies who have rigorously applied people analytics to guide their actions, and are holding senior executives to account for progress in building a winning gender-balanced business.

Case study: VW Group UK

VW Group UK (consisting of the brands Audi, VW, SEAT, Skoda and VW Commercial Vehicles) are adapting their business model to suit a rapidly changing environment. They are moving from producing cars to providing mobility services. This shift in purpose has led to the need for different skills, and has created the business case for a better gender balance in the business.

The company has increased year on year the representation of women in the lower quartiles of the business to create a gender-balanced pipeline. According to the gender pay gap data, in April 2019 women occupied 28% of the highest-paid jobs, 35% of the upper-middle quartile, 44% of the lower-middle quartile and 69% of the lowest-paid jobs. The hiring success in the lower quartiles has led to what is expected to be a temporary widening of the pay gap until a better gender balance is also achieved in the top quartile.

VW Group UK now have a goal to fill at least 30% of senior management roles (executive and direct reports combined) with women by 2021; accelerated from a previous target date of 2025. As of April 2020, they have reached 25% as a result of having 19% female representation in the top roles and 29% in the bigger pool of direct reports.

The HR team analyses the gender data by brand and function on a monthly basis and notes that progress is not always linear; due to the smaller number of top roles, the sensitivity to one or two women moving roles has high impact. Actions taken show the positive impact of people analytics, and effectively communicating information with decision makers. They share the data monthly to stimulate discussions with senior managers about key female talent, and have conversations with women to ascertain their personal career plans and then disseminate this information to internal HR groups to ensure they are aware of potential candidates for future opportunities. Although there is a hiring pause due to the impact of the pandemic, action is still being taken to nurture a pipeline of potential future hires through ensuring the recruitment team are fully briefed with hiring criteria, and maintaining connections with possible new or returning recruits through professional networks.

Mandatory gender-balanced shortlists have been introduced, but have revealed that (as with many businesses) managers are reluctant to hire a woman with potential and invest time and energy in her development rather than take a male counterpart (perhaps with lower potential but with more experience). This commonly occurring 'best for today' rather than 'best for tomorrow' mindset will be addressed through inclusive leadership workshops, and a process whereby managers with vacancies must justify the criteria they're identifying as an essential prerequisite. To celebrate those who do implement the gender-balance strategy, positive hiring examples will be showcased in the monthly gender KPIs update.

Penny Weatherup, HR Director, VW Group UK, notes: 'Monitoring our gender-balance data provides a platform to be absolutely transparent about our progress. Senior leaders must be aware of the data as a start point when hiring, relate it to their specific team gender balance and use it to challenge their own thinking. The data provides context to wider conversations about cultural change, e.g. diversity as a broader strategic topic and how greater diversity can advance the performance of the organization.'

It is clear that the success of VW Group UK's gender-balance strategy to date is due to an effective use of the data by senior executives to identify priorities and workable solutions.

Case study: Auto Trader Group plc

The FTSE 100 company Auto Trader Group plc is proud of their gender balance and diversity credentials. The COO, Catherine Faiers, is a Patron of the Automotive 30% Club and CEO Nathan Coe is a member of the Global 30% Club. The Chairman Ed Williams has always been very keen to have gender parity in the senior teams, and at the time of writing they are one of the few FTSE companies with 50% female representation on the board, 40% on the executive committee, 32% in their direct reports and an overall companywide female representation of 39%. Their gender pay gap report for 2019 shows 33.5% female representation in the highest-paid quartile, 28.7% in the upper-mid, 43.8% in the lower-mid and 49.2% in the lowest quartile.

Auto Trader has a very low attrition rate so the middle layers see little movement, and they have a higher number of men there because female recruits into technology roles are only relatively recent entry-level hires. This is a success story because much effort has been expended to attract more women and overcome the challenge of a limited pool of women with tech qualifications, resulting in the majority of graduate hires being female. They also introduced a re-training programme for people who want to change their career to digital and 60% of participants were women.

The Auto Trader data reporting system is a simple but effective download from the payroll system to a spreadsheet that removes anomalies, such as individuals on parental or maternity leave or salary sacrifice schemes. Their pay gap analysis process follows the Acas best practice guidelines. People analytics data including leaver questionnaires is collected by People analysts and shared with the board and senior leaders with suggestions for what action could be taken to address the gender gap. The data is also shared with the women's network for their input of ideas, in what is a great example of inclusive decision making.

The Auto Trader Group plc 2019 annual report boldly states: 'We won't be satisfied until we reach parity, and therefore remain dedicated to eliminating the gender pay gap completely. Our commitment that everyone has equal opportunities to reach their full potential remains in line with our focus to welcome more women into our business and to offer them exciting careers.'

Summary

It's essential to know your starting point, identify your end goal and plan how to get there via incremental short-term steps. You must examine the data to get to the real root cause of issues and identify priorities for action, applying problem-solving techniques rather than jumping to conclusions or solutioneering. Senior leaders must own the goals and be held to account for meeting them, and sufficient resources must be allocated to fund the changes that will lead to a significant return on the investment.

The next step is to cast your net wide and engage with new sources of skills to look for the best person for each job. You must not settle for simply hiring those who discovered your company; you must go and find those talented diverse women who might not even have you on their career radar. This is the focus of the next chapter.

10 Step 2: Reach out to new talent pools – Find new sources of skills

In Chapter 3, I outlined many reasons why businesses are competing in a race for skills, while hitting a perfect storm of issues that are working to make such skills scarcer. All of these factors mean we have to stay focused on attracting the very best talent, as we move to more efficient and productive ways of working with fewer but higher-skilled employees. You must plan for the future as well as fill vacancies today. Identify the skills you need for future business transformation and update job roles and person specifications to reflect this, ensuring that the criteria are not stereotypically male traits and also will not inadvertently limit the number of women who will meet them.

Then identify the potential sources of diverse women with these skills, both internal and external, and consider transferable skills from other departments or sectors. Reach out to women at the start of their career as well as those already in leadership roles. An employer with a gender imbalance either within the organization or specific job role is legally permitted to take positive action to increase the number of applications from women. They are not permitted to discriminate against men during the recruitment process, but they can increase the number of women they can select from. Unfortunately, confusion around equal opportunity legislation means many employers are reluctant to target schemes specifically at women even though they are perfectly entitled to do so.

I've found that female-only careers events are more successful than mixed-gender events for getting more engagement and active participation from young women in considering careers in traditionally male-dominated sectors. This is because in mixed events the men tend to dominate the conversation and the women get the impression the job is for the boys, not them.

Marc Benioff of Salesforce explains the importance of making the extra effort to ensure you get the best female talent:

> I don't believe we should be hiring any woman who applies simply for the sake of meeting a quota. But I do insist we go the extra mile to find those highly qualified women candidates who we believe would be the best fit for the role.[1]

There are several sources of female talent that you should reach out to:

o   Women within your company

o   Women who have left your company

o   Women returners

o   Professional women in sector and external networks

o   Young women in education

Let's look at each of these sources in turn.

Women within your company

Many organizations will employ higher numbers of women in occupations that are traditionally more attractive to them. There will be high-performing women in HR, training, finance, marketing and administrative roles. Development pathways could be created to enable them to move across functions into more operational roles or with profit and loss responsibility that are deemed as business critical and are important stepping stones to the top team. I personally moved from HR to sales within Ford and found the skill set employed to be virtually identical. Women need encouragement and support to move from a specialist function into a role that would give them more business leadership experience. This can be done successfully by making at least one cross-functional move the norm for all employees as they move up the career ladder.

Women who have left your company

Your organization will have invested significant amounts in the recruitment and development of female employees who then went on to exit the company. Their reasons for leaving will be many and varied, but is most likely to be due to a perceived lack of promotion prospects. A report by PwC in 2015 found that for both male and female job movers and job hunters, a lack of opportunities for career progression was cited as the top reason they decided to leave their former employers.[2]

Women have told me that they left due to an inflexibility of working hours leading to difficulties balancing work and home commitments, or because the manager they were working for at the time was incompetent. In your journey to become an inclusive organization, you will need to address these issues. Now is the time to reconnect with these women, many of whom will have joined other companies and climbed the career ladder to senior roles. You shouldn't hold a grudge over apparent disloyalty; it's likely they would have stayed had you had the conditions at the time in which they could thrive. Track down your female diaspora via LinkedIn and negotiate their return. Experience gained at a competitor or supplier could be extremely useful.

Women returners

According to a PwC report in 2016, a significant source of underutilized talent is professional women returning from career breaks. Seventy-six per cent of professional women on career breaks want to return to work, yet three in five highly skilled and qualified returning professional women could end up in lower-skilled, and as a result, lower-paid, jobs.[3]

These are women who have relevant experience and expertise in your sector (not necessarily your company) and have had a few years out of the working world. Traditional recruitment practices have discriminated against them due to the rejection of people with CV gaps. I have personal experience of this. Several years ago, I was headhunted for a role in an automotive manufacturer for a similar role to one I had held at Ford of Europe. I was on a career break with two young children and was not looking to return to corporate life but was intrigued when approached. However, the headhunter called and confided that the recruiting managers refused to look beyond the gap on my CV and that I was a mother, despite the headhunter pointing out that it was discriminatory. It made me wonder how many women actively applying to roles at that company were being rejected on discriminatory grounds.

It's a myth that women lose their skills and experience when they take a career break. In fact, they develop their skills even further: planning and scheduling, project management, team leadership, problem solving, crisis management and conflict resolution are all required of a primary carer of dependents. Creating an International Book Day costume for a young child with 12 hours' notice using only cardboard and Sharpie pens needs untold levels of creativity and ingenuity. Women who are forced to give up their job to facilitate the relocation of their family due to the promotion of their partner demonstrate significant skills when they take charge of managing the house move, finding new schools, and learning a new language if it is a foreign assignment.

An organization called Women Returners helps corporate employers tap into this talent pool through structured re-entry programmes, and has proved that such women only take a few weeks to perform to a high level in the new role. So all that's needed is a slightly longer induction period to enable them to familiarize themselves with updated office systems and protocols. Many women returners feel more comfortable returning in a role lower than they left; but employers should challenge this, because when their confidence quickly returns, they could be employed at least at the same level they left on.

You can find these women through organizations like Women Returners and also through professional connections on LinkedIn. You could also implement a recruitment campaign targeting them on social media.

Professional women in sector and external networks

There are many talented women in leadership roles that work for your competitors, or don't work in your sector but have transferable skills. These professionals may be looking for opportunities in organizations that have an inclusive culture and have made a firm commitment to improve the gender balance. Promote your inclusive values and the action you're taking to get a gender balance on social media platforms. Engage with women's networks and other professional networks to identify potential hires. Encourage your female leaders to take part in digital conferences, webinars and host virtual networking events to raise the visibility of the fact that women have a seat at the executive table in your company. Attracting top-performing women from one of your competitors will have the double impact of gaining a valuable resource as well as depriving your competitor of it.

In 2016, Kia UK started to sponsor the England women's cricket team and then also the Women's Cricket Super League. They further enhanced their reputation as supporters of women's sport in 2019 by sponsoring the Kia Summer Smash, a grassroots T10 competition for female club cricketers. This put the Kia brand firmly on the radar of women across the country and raised their brand awareness amongst a potential employee and customer audience.

Young women in education

It is important to build a female talent pipeline for the future, so encourage more young women to apply for roles in your business by positioning yourself as an inclusive employer of choice in the community, and build relationships with schools, colleges, girls' networks and local community groups or sports teams for girls.

> It's also important to present an authentic female face to university students to encourage them to join your company as graduates. PwC Germany implemented an Advisory Career Lounge on university campuses where female students could meet current female employees over drinks and snacks. This activity saw a 33% rise in the number of female applicants and a 42% rise in female campus hires.

Look to support activities that encourage more girls to consider careers in your industry, and to study relevant courses. As mentioned previously, career gender stereotypes are set by the age of eight years old, so it's essential to engage with primary schools to tackle stereotypes at a young age and encourage girls and boys to widen their career choices beyond outdated norms.

The case studies that follow give examples of two companies that are making their employer brands attractive to young women through outreach activities.

Case study: CDK Global (UK) Ltd

The technology company CDK Global (UK) Ltd has a senior leadership team that is 38% women, up from 12% in 2018, but this isn't the same picture across other regions. In 2019, a strategic decision was taken to improve this gender balance by joining the Automotive 30% Club and aiming for 30% of key roles to be filled by women by 2030. The Managing Director, Stuart Miles, is also a Patron of the club.

They decided to build CDK Global's reputation as an inclusive company that promotes opportunities for women, both in terms of opening opportunities for future talent, but also for supporting existing employees and leaders. They invested in outreach activities to support the female talent pipeline in automotive and technology by raising awareness and educating school, college and university students on the diverse opportunities that exist for young women to pursue.

One key activity was to sponsor the Automotive 30% Club Outreach Network (now rebranded as the Inspiration for Innovation Network), which empowered CDK Global's employees to engage with youngsters in schools as role models. This sponsorship also enabled other companies to participate along with CDK Global in three large-scale events in schools, and develop their outreach activities as a collective goal to improve awareness of careers in the automotive industry, especially for female students. The events delivered a transformative experience to 700 youngsters, and 84% of them stated afterwards that they had a greater understanding of the importance of a gender-balanced workforce.

CDK Global's volunteers were highly motivated by the outreach activities and the experience of engaging with students helped them with professional development. Furthermore, many of the volunteers have since been involved in panel debates and open discussions to raise the voice of women and awareness of challenges internally. The sponsorship has been a catalyst for more regular discussions at executive leadership level with opportunities for women at CDK Global now a key part of the business agenda moving forward.

Additional outreach activities that took place as a result of the sponsorship included a Personal Brand Masterclass for young Girlguiding Advocates, a motivational speech to female engineers at Imperial College, a speech to the

Women's Economics Society at the University of Edinburgh, and six Volvo, Toyota and Kia volunteers took the role of mentors in the Girls' Day School Trust Techathon with 100 girls from 22 schools. Each volunteer engagement mentioned CDK as the sponsor of their appearance and was supported by posts on social media.

Stuart Miles, Managing Director, UK&I, CDK Global (UK) Ltd, notes: 'We are delighted to have the opportunity to work with so many young people at a crucial stage in their development. The Outreach Network allows CDK Global and partner companies to showcase what a career in automotive and technology really looks like. Women currently hold 17% of tech roles and 16% of automotive roles in the UK. If we want to continue to innovate in the future with fresh ideas, we need to redress this balance and build a diverse workforce.'

Case study: Bentley Motors Ltd

The luxury car manufacturer Bentley Motors Ltd is part of the global VW Group and so shares the group's gender-balance and diversity ambitions but operates as a separate entity to VW Group UK. Like many other automotive manufacturing companies with production and engineering functions, the workforce and leadership are predominantly male. Bentley Motors is committed to addressing the gender balance and reducing the gap and saw their median pay gap reduce in 2019 for the third consecutive year to 4.7%, quite an achievement compared to the UK average of 17.3%.

According to their 2019 gender pay gap report, they have 15% female representation in the highest-paid quartile (a 7% increase since 2017), 16% in the upper-middle quartile, 17% in the lower-middle and 23% in the lowest-paid quartile.

Bentley Motors' current goal is to increase the percentage of women in management to 20% by 2025. They are committed to encouraging women from all backgrounds into the automotive industry and are supporting many programmes and initiatives that give women the opportunity to explore the industry and the wide variety of roles within manufacturing, engineering and digital technology.

Dr Astrid Fontaine, member of the board for People, IT and Digitalisation, is a Patron of the Automotive 30% Club, and has made a public commitment to aim for 30% female representation in key leadership roles by 2030. Bentley Motors hope to have a class-leading gender balance amongst their peers, through attracting talented women and then supporting and promoting them.

According to Dr Fontaine: 'The automotive sector has traditionally been very male dominated, but there is clear evidence that businesses with a gender balance perform higher than less diverse companies. The same research suggests that a gender balance helps improve access to future talent, enhances decision making and is associated with deeper levels of consumer insight and employee engagement.'

Bentley Motors sees partnerships with education as a key opportunity to attract more women into the business, and provide students and graduates with placement and work opportunities. Dr Astrid Fontaine has appeared as a role model keynote speaker at events to encourage girls into STEM, and schools, colleges and universities, and has hosted a workplace visit for school girls as part of the Automotive 30% Club's outreach activities. Bentley Motors is collaborating with the local university technical college (UTC) in Crewe to encourage more young women to consider careers in engineering and technology.

To celebrate International Women's Day, Bentley Motors ran an online campaign showcasing their senior female leaders and women in roles that break traditional stereotypes, and the company participates in various initiatives across the industry to encourage the next generation of women, such as Great British Women in Automotive and the Inspiring Automotive Women Awards.

As a result of the outreach activities to encourage more female applicants, 67% of the digital apprentices recruited in 2019 were women. This has led to an overall 24% increase in female representation in the company's total apprentice population.

Summary

There are many deep pools of diverse talented women both within your company and beyond. Succession planning policies should be innovative and creative, and include cross-functional moves. Your future female sales director could currently be working in training. You should look to hire in at all management levels and not just at the entry level, and attract women with expertise in running business units. Enticing a top performer away from a competitor helps you and hinders them. It is important to realize that company policies that prohibit external recruitment, such as hiring freezes, could damage your plans to achieve a gender balance. If your internal female pool is small or relatively new and inexperienced, it will take a long time for them to move up the pipeline, so it's essential to be able to look externally if you are unable to develop gender-balanced shortlists from internal candidates.

Having identified the various places where you can look for the best person for each job, before you hire them you must ensure that your organization is calibrated effectively to ensure they will be fully included. The next chapter explains how.

11 Step 3: Recalibrate for inclusion – Design for productivity not presenteeism

You can set targets, make declarations of intent, be inclusive leaders, recruit more women, but if you don't ensure the organization is designed to focus on productivity and outputs rather than presenteeism, and ensure women are not excluded from participation, very little progress will be made in terms of retaining and promoting them. The organizations we work in today are not designed to deliberately exclude women, but because they were originally designed to suit a particular profile of man there will still be practices and protocols in place that will create a barrier to female participation (and also many young men with different lifestyles to their fathers). Organizational structures, jobs, policies and processes must be consciously designed for inclusion, and working norms must drive inclusive behaviour.

Exclusion can take place in many forms, some of it due to decisions and policies to keep women out of a man's profession, some of it down to false assumptions about women, and often through inadvertently excluding them by upholding systems that are designed for men and simply don't accommodate women.

One hundred and fifty years ago, the 'Edinburgh Seven' were the first UK women to attend medical school. They faced extreme hostility from male students and teachers who wanted to keep women out. They were all denied the ability to graduate or qualify as doctors, and had to go to universities in Bern or Paris to be awarded their medical doctorates. Due to their perseverance, however, the door was opened for future generations of women to enter the profession.

In 1991, 55 years after Sabiha Gökçen became the first female combat pilot for the Turkish airforce, Julie Anne Gibson became the first female UK RAF pilot. A few years ago, I was fortunate to sit next to Jo Salter at dinner, the first female fast jet pilot, appointed in 1992. She shared that the reason women hadn't been permitted to fly fast jets before was that UK officers couldn't imagine what a woman would do if she needed to urinate (the men peed into a tube). So she introduced them to sanitary towels. British women had been barred from the role for years simply because of toilet etiquette.

Looking through a 21st-century lens, it's hard to believe that women faced such exclusion, through intention or ignorance. You must scrutinize the practices you have in your business to ensure it's not still happening under the radar, leading to women being excluded from roles or being unable to thrive in the working environment.

There are a number of places to look:

o   Facilities and conditions

o   Working norms

o   Meeting protocols

o   Competition and risk

o   Organization structure

Let's explore each one.

Facilities and conditions

I don't often talk about toilets but here we go again. It's a signal that the place isn't designed for women if they don't have toilet facilities in the same number or proximity as men. When Ford of Britain appointed its first female director a few years ago, they had to install female toilets on the executive floor. Workshops in car dealerships often have only male toilets, forcing female technicians to use customer facilities further away. This not only implies female technicians don't need to be catered for; it also impacts on their efficiency score because it takes them off the job for longer. One thing that's guaranteed to annoy women is to provide male-only toilets alongside unisex toilets (often also for disabled people), but no female-only toilets. A man can go in either but a woman can only go in one so has half the provision, and without going into too much detail about what goes on in the loo, women take longer for a variety of reasons and so will end up queueing. So make sure you invest in the basics to make it clear women are not simply an afterthought.

Employers must invest in the necessary PPE, clothing and equipment to enable men and women to perform all roles safely and, most importantly, ensure its efficacy isn't reduced by it not fitting properly. Don't have a sexist dress code, such as expecting women to wear a skirt rather than trousers. Dress codes must not be a source of harassment by colleagues or customers, so any requirements on women to dress in a sexual or provocative way are unlawful. Any requirement for women to wear high heels, make-up, skirts, have manicured nails, certain hairstyles or specific types of hosiery are gender-specific prescriptive requirements and will also be unlawful. To be on the right side of the law, and to ensure women feel comfortable at work, always apply the same code to men and women.

Women will frequently complain that rooms are too cold, and large conference rooms with air conditioning are like a fridge. A jumper can be donned but it's hard to work in gloves. A study published in the scientific journal Nature Climate Change found that women prefer a temperature of 24°C, whereas men prefer 21. It claimed that the majority of office buildings use temperatures that were set with men in mind. The 'thermal comfort model' that sets the ideal temperature for air conditioners and central heating systems was developed back in the 1960s, using Fanger's Thermal Comfort model through an analysis of the resting weight of a 69kg 40-year-old male.[1] Research published in 2019 by the University of Southern California found that increasing the temperature to 24°C and above increased women's productivity. The relationship between temperature and performance was much less dramatic in men, so if you're aiming for a gender-balanced productive work balance, remove this impediment and turn up the thermostat.[2]

Working norms

I've been asked to 'find women who are prepared to work a 60-hour week in the workplace like men'. As a self-confessed workaholic, I can see the temptation to expect this of all colleagues. However, it's clear that few people stay productive through such a long working week, and that's equally true for men and women. The difference is presenteeism; I've observed that more men than women are willing to give the impression of working long hours due to being visibly available, but that doesn't mean that they're producing more than their peers. I've known more than one male manager to go home but leave his suit jacket on his chair and computer switched on to give the appearance they were working late.

People have different styles of working that can lead to good results. Some can achieve more in a single conversation with a customer than another person can in a day's correspondence. Some can write a communication so succinctly that readers immediately understand, whereas others need to spend hours on clarification. The real issue is why anyone would accept hours apparently worked, rather than the level and quality of outputs, as the measure of productivity.

Most organizations still adopt a working model that reflects life of a century ago, with attendance required in the workplace so that managers can observe the employees, with official start and finish times. The world has changed, and the mass adoption of digital technology has led to different human behaviour. Work tasks have been automated, work effort can be monitored through digital systems, communications between staff and customers can take place remotely, and a growing need to be open for business almost 24/7 to match customer buying behaviour has led to a variety of shifts and working patterns.

The employees of the 21st century are very different in terms of gender, ethnicity, religion and family obligations, and the working model designed for the traditional default male is no longer fit for purpose. If your organization maintains outdated patterns, you will fail to attract talented people because they are unable to thrive in that environment.

An important breakthrough is the adoption of flexible and agile working. It's well documented that women place a premium on flexibility over other aspects, because for some women it's the only way they can access work due to caring obligations. However, PwC found in their 2017 report that flexible work arrangements and a culture of work–life balance was in the top three most important criteria for selecting a job *for both men and women* (along with competitive salary and career progression).[3] To attract the brightest talent, employers need to make flexible and remote working part of their employer brand, and those who select it must have the same pay or career prospects as others. Former Unilever Chair and CEO, Niall FitzGerald, addressed this during his tenure, and claimed that he used the principle that every job can be operated in a flexible manner unless it could be demonstrably proven otherwise.

So through behavioural design, changing the default to flexible working, and forcing an opt-out rather than an opt-in, more workers will take it up. If it's no longer a woman's issue, it shouldn't lead to gender-specific career penalties. Flexibility becomes the default. It becomes 'pay for performance, not face time'.

Work must be repositioned to be *what* we do, not *where* we go. Remote or 'hybrid' or 'blended' working (combining some days in the office with some at home) will enable more women to access fulfilling careers. People management processes that set clear work goals and quality standards, and assess achievement against them, will result in higher productivity because the employee knows exactly what needs to be done and can plan their schedule effectively. There are many digital systems available to make work tasks transparent to all team members, and to ensure effective communications, so their physical location becomes irrelevant.

As well as benefiting women and men, remote working has other advantages for the business. It saves money due to reduced energy usage, work-related travel, and IT and real estate costs. It can enable companies to secure skilled talent in less competitive and lower-cost locations, and could improve employment rates in less economically active areas. A London company could have a remote worker based in Liverpool. So, it's not surprising that in a recent Gartner Group study, 74% of CFOs said they will make remote work a permanent part of their cost-management plans.[4] It can save your employees money too; a study of 2,500 US knowledge workers conducted by Citrix and the Centre of Economics and Business Research (Cebr) in 2019 found that employees working remotely just two days per week would save over $107 billion, largely based on reduced fuel and commuting costs.[5]

The majority of employees with a job that can be done remotely are more productive and work equal or longer hours when working remotely. A One-Poll survey of 10,000 global employees for Citrix found that the majority of respondents reported they are more focused and productive working from home (62% in the UK), and the majority said they work the same or more hours as when in the office (68.2% of UK respondents).[6] This is due to the shorter distance from bed to desk, along with fewer interruptions from colleagues. If you're afraid that a certain worker would be binge-watching their favourite shows, then that worker is just as likely to be avoiding work in the office and distracting others while they do. Those that cannot work as effectively are likely to be living in unsuitable accommodation for home working, or at the time of the survey may have been distracted by childcare or homeschool obligations due to school closures.

Despite often working longer hours, remote workers have a healthier work–life balance because they have the flexibility to manage their personal lives while working. Overall, remote workers say they are less stressed and can focus and get their work done faster.

In their April 2020 paper, Titan Alon, Matthias Doepke, Jane Olmstead-Rumsey and Michèle Tertilt state that more men in the US are currently in jobs that can be done flexibly and remotely but choose not to, and fewer women are, but more choose to. They remain hopeful that the pandemic could lead to more men choosing to work remotely in future, removing the career penalty it currently gives to women.[7] The new working norms that require productivity rather than presenteeism should be the default setting from now on and will help achieve a gender balance.

Meeting protocols

Group dynamics in the meeting room favour the more vocal and assertive participants, and in predominantly male companies this is usually the men. People choose their seating position relative to the boss and their own perceived status. This is a manifestation of competition, and since their school years, women have not been as competitive in mixed-sex environments as they are in all-female company. I have observed this at work and in outreach events with schools, and it seems to start when children are about eight years old.

It's essential to include everyone in the discussion, using effective chairing and meeting protocols that enable all to be heard, and outlaw interruptions and stealing the limelight. Coupled with this should be the awareness that those being interrupted or ignored are more likely to be women and people of colour who are a minority. Video meetings help because they eliminate seating positions, everyone is equally visible and everyone can be heard.

As well as including people equitably, you must avoid excluding people from meetings. This could be due to the location, time and length it's scheduled (early morning, late afternoon or on the day a flexible worker has off). Best practice being implemented in many companies as a result of the pandemic is to default to all meetings continuing with all participants on video call, no matter where they are. Previously, when only a small number of people dialled or video linked in, it was easy for those in the room to forget about digital participants. It is much better to put everyone in one virtual space so no one is overlooked, meaning that even if some people are able to attend physically it's better that they don't unless everyone can.

Competition and risk

Women may avoid companies and roles where they feel they're not fully able to influence the outcome of their efforts due to sharp competitive practices or presenteeism. Women are usually raised to avoid competition with men, and will be more risk averse than men often due to a heightened awareness of negative consequences. As a result, they may choose jobs with more stable and predictable reward systems.

A 2004 study by Uwe Jirjahn and Gesine Stephan found that women tend to self-select into pay schemes whereby they are paid for specific tangible outputs or finished articles rather than time worked (piece rate schemes); this is less frequent amongst men.[8] This is because the performance measures are transparent, objective and based on actual outputs. Time-wage regimes that pay by the hour, week or month without tangible outputs and with subjective performance measures are less attractive because they leave more room for discrimination or unconscious bias.

Competitive salary schemes against colleagues are even less appealing. A 2010 study by Jeffrey Flory, Andreas Leibbrandt and John List found that women avoid competitive salary schemes, whereas men also dislike them but still apply. Women were more likely to apply to fixed-salary roles and less likely to apply for jobs where compensation was dependent on competitive job performance. The variation was also there but not as great with men. Interestingly, there is a difference if the compensation is based on team success; women are more likely than men to opt for a competitive salary scheme if it has team-based rewards, whereas men are more likely than women to opt for rewards based on individual performance. Women have more confidence of a successful outcome if they're in a group, but men tend to doubt their team members' abilities.[9]

Commission-based remuneration systems that shift the business risk onto the employee, and can damage teamwork, productivity, profitability and customer satisfaction due to the intra-team competition they generate, should be replaced with objectives and clear and fair expectations of output in return for the salary. This would attract a more diverse pool of recruits for sales roles.

It's important to realize that the context of the competition is critical. Studies by Uri Gneezy, Kenneth Leonard and John List with the Khasi in North East India, where women are the heads of households, found them to be far more competitive against men than the women in patriarchal societies like ours.[10] Also, in stereotypical female skill areas such as verbal tasks, women are generally more willing to compete against men. Women are also more comfortable competing against women than they are men, and this is reinforced through gender-segregated sports teams.

John Coates examined the impact of success and failure on risk taking in his 2012 book and found a critical difference between men and women due to testosterone levels. He measured the biochemical responses of traders in 'moments of transformation' after wins and losses. Male winners show heightened levels of testosterone, which has been found to increase an appetite for risk, while in male losers it was reduced. So the more successful men are, the more risks they take. The more they fail, the more risk averse they become. Women don't have the same levels of testosterone and don't display this boom and bust approach to risk.[11] Some academics have suggested that employing more female traders would avoid bubbles in financial markets.

We need environments that include different risk types so we need both men and women in teams to achieve a balanced approach to risk. If your business seeks employees with a high propensity for risk then you will attract and retain fewer women, and your company leaders may not be making carefully processed wise decisions.

Organization structure

Command and control management styles and hierarchical military-type structures stifle creativity and fail to utilize the organization's collective intelligence. The taller the structure, the more there is a power imbalance, and the more women are likely to be invisible under the many management layers. Flatter structures and inclusive decision making leads to more success and collaboration both within and across teams.

I've observed that women leave large corporations with these traditional structures and thrive in smaller organizations where their contribution is more visible and they can play a wider, more influential role. This is due to the power being more evenly balanced throughout the organization, or in the case of the female entrepreneur, largely in their own hands.

The following case studies provide some good examples of designing the organization for productivity rather than presenteeism, and so creating an environment in which a much wider variety of people of both sexes can thrive.

Case study: Jardine Motors Group

Jardine Motors Group employs 3,000 people across 60 dealerships in the UK. It achieved 30% female representation at senior manager level in 2019. The company has 12.9% female representation in the highest pay quartile, 19.7% in the upper-mid quartile, 43% in the lower-mid quartile and 34.4% in the lowest pay quartile. Jardine Motors Group has committed to achieve at least 30% of the key leadership roles in all levels of the business to be filled by women by 2030.

Prior to the pandemic, remote and flexible working was encouraged but only some employees adopted it. Many managers thought homeworking meant their team would be less productive, less engaged or would struggle to align with the business's operational needs. However, this is no longer the case. As part of the phased return to work, they've identified a number of teams and roles where working from home will be the default setting. The company has had great success with working from home during lockdown and is accelerating plans to create a longer-term formalized policy, recognizing that it helps colleagues who need flexibility.

Presenteeism no longer determines a colleague's performance and instead managers are focused on output and impact. The company invested in Microsoft Office 365 last year and since then has been rolling out Teams, SharePoint and Yammer to keep colleagues engaged, connected and to facilitate collaborative working. The use of Teams in particular has meant they're able to broaden and diversify those involved in meetings and conversations. They're no longer restricted by travel times restricting diary availability, and work in a more agile manner.

They recognize though that working remotely can affect people's wellbeing, so as part of their on-going focus on mental health, they start each meeting with a chance for colleagues to talk about how they're actually feeling, and share any concerns or anxieties.

A successful meeting in a virtual or physical setting relies on the effectiveness of the chairperson. Jardine Motors Group already had an established protocol to ensure everyone shares their updates without interruption, questions are asked at the end, and there's a closing check out where colleagues can share final thoughts.

This eliminates any tendency for women and ethnic minority representatives to be talked over or not listened to. Using technology to hold meetings simply builds on these existing ways of working.

They've observed that whereas confidence can be a barrier to participation in physical meetings, people are more willing to speak in virtual meetings. Technology is flattening their hierarchical structures, because it's clear colleagues feel more confident and less intimidated when a senior person is present virtually rather than physically. Due to this, the company will continue to hold meetings digitally even if social distancing regulations are relaxed. To enable all with caring duties to participate, daily meetings don't start before 10am.

Customer purchase behaviours are changing, demonstrating a desire to engage with the business beyond usual working hours and wanting to connect digitally. This demands a more flexible approach to work patterns. Working from home helps to achieve this because it suits both the colleague and the customer.

Back-to-back digital discussions can be more exhausting than physical meetings. New protocols have therefore been established to ensure people manage their time effectively. These include 'meeting-free Fridays', a late start or early finish at least one day a week for family time and planned lunch breaks. Senior executives set a good example by adhering to these new procedures. Team-building activities take place during the core working day so no one is excluded. There is also encouragement for people to take time to switch off; working from home saves valuable time usually lost to commuting, but the commute often served the purpose of decompressing after work. Colleagues are advised to find another way of achieving this before going straight into the family setting.

Jardine Motors Group has also introduced a number of best practices to achieve women's inclusion. Their 'Women in JMG' network brings together female colleagues and male allies to tackle barriers to career progression. They have robust succession planning and talent planning processes, and key metrics to monitor gender balance are reviewed each quarter with senior executives to identify rising female talent, and participate in a cross-company mentoring scheme. They have implemented a new performance review process that ensures the right support is in place to help colleagues with their career development, identifying short and long-term career goals. The company also recently revamped their learning and development programmes using an online platform in recognition of the difficulty many women faced in accessing courses away from home.

Case study: Volvo Car UK

Volvo is committed to creating more flexible working opportunities for their people and prospective candidates and is embarking on a number of initiatives to support this. They believe this will provide a better work–life balance and offer more choices, together with opening up employment opportunities further and to a more diverse audience. As of July 2020, they have 43% female representation (three in seven) within the executive management team. As a member of the Automotive 30% Club, they have made a public commitment to achieve at least 30% of key leadership roles to be filled by diverse women by 2030.

They're committed to moving away from the traditional office approach to work and office hours, and are redesigning their office space and practices to encourage more activity-based and blended working opportunities. During 2020, they actively encouraged the use of a wider range of flexible working opportunities to enable their people to select the option that works both for them and the organization. The company is using technology to support remote working and maintain cohesion, and their weekly updates and corporate communication updates are recorded and broadcast to ensure all employees are kept up to date on strategy and progress. They've also increased the number of wellbeing initiatives this year and moved them online to allow everyone to benefit from them.

Volvo Car UK will introduce a new approach to their performance management and competency framework during 2020, which encourages more regular conversation and feedback loops, with a focus on outputs. They have successfully launched other key initiatives to drive diversity and inclusion, including an enhanced family policy to support new parents and a female mentoring programme that includes individuals at all levels from a number of different countries.

Summary

So remember, you must consciously design your organization for inclusion of women and minority groups, and ensure you don't have systems in place that inadvertently exclude them. Ensure working conditions are favourable for both sexes and that practices nudge people to adopt the required norms and inclusive behaviours, avoiding impression management, presenteeism and damaging internal competition. When you have recalibrated the workplace for inclusion you will be ready to recruit and welcome in the women. The next chapter will provide tips on how to do this effectively.

12 Step 4: Welcome in the women – Recruit equitably

So you've analysed your data, identified the priority roles you need to go fast first with and reached out to the female talent pool you wish to attract. Now you should turn to scrutinizing your recruitment and selection processes and monitor success rates by gender and ethnicity at each stage to ensure there's no bias built into a particular step.

You must examine your job descriptions and adverts to make sure they don't accidentally alienate your ideal candidates, and promote your vacancies where women will actually see them, including those who are not actively job seeking. Design induction programmes to make women feel welcome, particularly if they are trailblazing by entering an environment with few female colleagues.

To welcome in the women by removing bias and barriers you should do the following:

o   Scrutinize selection data

o   Be transparent about pay

o   Be blind to gender and diversity cues

o   Remove higher hurdles

o   Don't confuse experience with expertise
o   Put two in a pool
o   Be careful with cultural fit
o   Hire in group cohorts
o   Learn the right language

Scrutinize selection data

Design recruitment and selection processes through a diversity lens, scrutinizing how different populations perform in different activities. If any task results in a particularly low or high relative performance by a specific group, then there's likely to be bias in it that is disproportionately affecting them. Panel interviews are an activity that should be avoided in selection processes due to group dynamics leading to the most powerful interviewer making the decision and others falling in line. Instead, do individual interviews by a diverse range of multiple assessors and compare the results.

I've hired hundreds and assessed thousands of applicants. However, the experience of hiring workers for Ford Motor Company in my early career shaped my understanding of the importance of scrutinizing data for bias in recruitment. It was 1994 and Ford was pursuing a globalization strategy, opening assembly operations across the world and shipping vehicles to them in 'knock-down' form like giant IKEA flat-packs. I was the Employee Relations Officer for KD Operations on the Dagenham estate when the call came to grow it to an operation ten times its size, and swiftly hire 150 more workers.

The existing KD workers were mainly white men. This didn't reflect the gender or ethnicity mix in the surrounding community, so I advertised roles in a range of locations, including corner shops. I designed an assessment centre with several activities rather than the usual interview, and monitored each stage for gender and ethnicity: applications received, candidates' post screening, invitations to the selection day, actual attendees at the selection day, success rates for each activity and successes and rejections from the selection day. I decided we wouldn't use any one of the activities to screen out, but use the overall success across them.

I was asked to accept the famous Ford Dagenham sewing machinists. In 1968, these trailblazing women had gone on strike asking for job grade parity with men operating machinery. They were given a pay increase and the strike paved the way for the Equal Pay Act 1970, but the women didn't get the new grade until after another strike in 1984. Their jobs were later outsourced, and attempts made to allocate them other roles at their new grade level. Ten years later, around 30 women were still unplaced because they didn't want production line roles. I was careful to ensure they went through the same selection process as other candidates to avoid any accusations of positive discrimination.

Through data analysis I found the white male candidates scored well at interview, but worse in the work sample and reasoning tests than female and BAME peers. This was because some had more interview experience, but also the interview with the foremen was the only subjective part of the process so there was a chance that bias crept in. Had the interview been used to screen out, we would have ended up with a predominantly white male cohort, some of whom might have struggled with the job practicalities or had poor numeracy and literacy. Using the results of all the activities with a pass rate for each one led to the selection of a diverse cohort with a much improved gender balance.

We recruited two-thirds of the sewing machinists, and they liked the piecework nature of the role. Their prowess at the physical work sample test meant that their male co-workers respected that they had not simply been token hires and had got the jobs for the right reasons.

Be transparent about pay

We often advertise roles with the term 'competitive salary' but how does a candidate know the market rate if she's working in a different sector? A director's pay could be £30,000 or £300,000 depending on the size of the company and the role. Job descriptions often make the job sound grander and higher status than it actually is. People use salary as the main indicator to assess if they're at the level of performance the job needs. Women are less likely to apply for a role where the salary isn't transparent because they may overestimate the competence required for a job, are less likely to take the risk of being rejected if they're uncertain about the status of the role and are less likely to think they will be successful in a salary negotiation than a man.

Women are also aware that a lack of transparency in salaries is a major cause of the gender pay gap, which is exacerbated by paying an increase on the candidate's previous earnings, rather than paying them a salary equal to that of their new peers. So women who may have been paid below the market rate in a previous company will continue to earn less than their new team members. This often works in the reverse for men, who may have negotiated hard and could be hired on salaries higher than their new peers. A 2016 study by Benjamin Artz, Amanda H. Goodall and Andrew J. Oswald found that women do in fact now try to negotiate pay but are always less successful than men because companies more readily accommodate a man's demands.[1]

Be blind to gender and diversity cues

One way of preventing bias entering the process is to ensure that recruiters are not aware of the gender and ethnicity of the applicant; so they may imagine they're reading about a white man.

The famous Boston Symphony Orchestra 1952 case study tells the story that the orchestra recruitment committee asked performers to play anonymously behind a screen in order to remove gender bias by their judges. At first it seemed to have no effect. Then someone noticed that the click-clack of high heels preceded the performance of each woman, so asked them to remove their shoes before entering. By removing this extra gender cue, far more women passed the auditions, and this has influenced the way musicians are selected the world over.

The most obvious gender and ethnicity cues are physical appearance and name. In order to remove the negative impact of the cues, redact them from application forms. Digital systems including Applied, GapJumpers and Unitive, are available to be used by employers to remove demographic data from CVs. Employers tell me that many more women and ethnic minority applicants get through the screening stage when blind hiring processes are used, even when the recruiting managers truly believe they have no bias. Prejudice is of course a key factor though. An HR manager confided that when she challenged a manager on exactly why he had rejected a particular applicant when he knew their name, but then accepted the same person when the name was redacted, he simply said he would never be able to learn to pronounce a foreign-sounding name so always screened those out.

Remove higher hurdles

Don't lower the performance standard expected to enable a woman to fill a role; to do so is totally unnecessary and would be patronizing and sexist. However, you must recognize that some applicants face higher hurdles than others, many of which are left there out of habit rather than being an indicator of effectiveness in the job.

Screening out people with a gap in the CV is a legacy from when candidates were mainly men and a gap was viewed with suspicion because it indicated a lack of employability, or being fired. Women are more likely to have breaks to raise children, and also have short gaps due to leaving work situations they found unendurable in a hurry, such as instances of being sexually harassed. As more men and women are choosing a non-linear approach to a career, with time out for travelling, caring or further study, a CV gap shouldn't be seen as a negative, but something to explore. It's likely that the applicant will have developed some useful transferable skills during that time out of employment.

When looking for trailblazer women to join stereotypically male organizations, don't ask for a passion for the product or sector. I run a search and selection programme for motor trade apprentices, and have placed many youngsters into fulfilling roles who had never considered the sector until we arrived at their school. I know many successful automotive leaders with little interest in cars but an enthusiasm for running a business and serving customers.

There's a social expectation that boys will be more capable with construction and mechanical tasks, but it's likely that they simply had more chance to practise. In a discussion with a group of potential apprentices, a young man shared that he'd already stripped a gearbox down with his uncle. A young woman exclaimed she would have loved the chance to do that. A standard selection process would have given him extra points for the experience; but it was an unfair advantage over the woman who had not had the same opportunity. The best selection process for youngsters is an extended work sample test in the form of a week of work experience. Both youngsters in the story passed their work experience week with flying colours and were hired as apprentice technicians. If the woman had applied elsewhere, it's possible that the lack of evidence of prior interest on her CV would have meant she was screened out at the first stage.

Another hurdle is using unnecessary criteria that narrow the applicant pool to a small population, or those prepared to ignore the criteria. As mentioned in Chapter 7, men are much more likely to apply for roles where they don't meet the criteria than women, and sometimes they get the job despite not meeting the criteria simply because they were the best from the small bunch that applied. This is a possible reason behind the 'there are no available women' excuse for a gender imbalance. Never use criteria that you're willing to walk away from when no one meets them.

Don't confuse experience with expertise

It's standard protocol to ask for three or five years' experience in a role, rather than seeking evidence for the level of expertise in the skills the job tenure represents. Yet we all know people who ace their job within six months and are ready for promotion in two years, when others may take five years to reach the same competence. Requiring the candidate to have stayed years in a job is effectively showing a preference for a plodder.

Conflating experience with expertise is a lazy approach to recruitment. Richness and depth of experience is often not related to time, and will have been gained in another company with different performance standards, promotional opportunities and organizational context that you can't draw a relevant comparison with.

If you're trying to encourage women to be trailblazers and break into roles that have previously been male domains, you can't demand years of previous experience because they won't have it, but the right woman could well outperform experienced peers after a few short months. Use a work sample test, look for evidence of transferable skills and an awareness of the job context and challenges through an explanation of how they would set about the job in their first 100 days. This will help you to assess potential to perform for you, rather than hearing about their performance in another company.

It's a known phenomenon that men are hired on future potential whereas women have to provide more past evidence of performance. This is because not enough recruiters have a vast number of female role models to draw upon to make them feel comfortable to assume a woman has the potential to perform at a senior level. Men therefore enjoy the ability of standing on the shoulders of the men who have gone before them, whereas women do not. A woman will often be expected to do lateral moves to prove her competence again before she is promoted.

Most companies have their best female representation at lower levels because they've ensured in recent years that entry-level hires are gender balanced. The way to fast track women to fill the gender gap in middle management is to remove the need for years of experience from all candidates and replace it with actual performance indicators. This removes the advantage that time-served mediocre male candidates have, replacing it with criteria that the best performers of any gender will have.

Put two in a pool

Stephanie Johnson, David Hekman and Elsa Chan found in their 2016 study that if there's only one woman in a candidate pool, there's statistically no chance she'll be hired. They established that a candidate pool of two women and two men led to a 50% chance of a woman being hired. Hiring was proportionate to the female representation in the pool. But when there was only one woman and three men, there was actually 0% chance she would be hired. A lone woman in the pool was never recruited; whereas a lone man led to a disproportionate 33% chance of the man being hired, rather than the 25% you would expect.[2]

The researchers suggest this is because people have a bias towards the status quo. If the job attracts a shortlist with a greater number of male candidates, then a single woman in the pool stands out as a deviation from the norm, and recruiters make a decision in line with the accepted norm. When the job attracts equal numbers of men and women, then the status quo becomes that the job could fit either and so the chances of success are equal for both sexes. When the job attracts more women than men though, the recruiters still have a legacy of wider experience of successful male candidates than female, so the man still stands a better chance. The data provides evidence that unbalanced shortlists disproportionately favour men.

The simple hack of always having gender-balanced shortlists, and including at least two women in recruitment pools, could have a significant impact on whether more women are successful based on their own performance, because they're no longer seen as a deviation from the male norm.

Be careful with cultural fit

Companies wish to hire recruits that are a good fit, and reflect the company values and ideal character traits. It's essential therefore that the values are inclusive and the traits are not just stereotypically male. Gender mix and diversity gives the fresh perspectives and ideas that lead to superior results, while recruiting to a narrowly defined specification will exclude different profiles to the historic norm unless they're designed for inclusion.

There's evidence of 'confirmatory categorization' in recruitment. This is when a candidate fits an imagined type or profile of person, usually like a successful previous incumbent that fitted well with the culture. Person specifications are written with that person in mind, and if that person was a white man there's likely to be a preference, possibly unconscious, to repeat the successful appointment. Recruiters experience dissonance with candidates who don't fit the same profile and find it difficult to move beyond it. Selectors will sometimes overlook specific job criteria or actually change it to fit the preferred male candidate that seems to embody the right character traits. Suddenly having worked abroad is seen as more useful than having led a project; yet the latter was one of the criteria on the job ad and the former wasn't.

To overcome the cloning conundrum, ensure leadership traits and person specifications are not stereotypically male. Also, make female leaders very visible. This could help create a corporate memory bank of successful diverse women to draw upon when imagining future leaders. It dispels the myth that few women make it to the top, and also helps to attract women to your company.

Hire in group cohorts

When hiring in cohorts, recruiters can compare the wide variety of applicants against each other and not traditional stereotypes or previous incumbents of a single role. There is a large pool of candidates to select from and compare to each other for several jobs, rather than only a few candidates for a single job, and this seems to enable the selection of a diverse group of recruits. Due to this, it is easier for companies to tackle the gender balance at entry level through hiring groups of graduates or apprentices.

Learn the right language

Research by the online jobs board Adzuna revealed that 60% of businesses showed male bias in the wording of their job adverts.[3] It was based on a study by Danielle Gaucher, Justin Friesen and Aaron Kay, which found job descriptions with masculine wording were less appealing to women. It wasn't that female candidates assumed they weren't up to the job, but the way the company and job was described didn't appeal to them so they didn't feel they'd belong there. Unconsciously, the women were reacting to the stereotypical associations of the words.[4]

According to Gaucher, Friesen and Kay, popular recruiting adjectives such as 'ambitious, assertive, decisive, determined and self-reliant' are seen as male gendered. To attract women, recruitment adverts should use more female-gendered words, like 'committed, connect, interpersonal and responsible'. In a male-gendered job description, a company might be described as 'a dominant engineering firm that boasts many clients', whereas the female-gendered version would read 'we are a community of engineers who have effective relationships with many satisfied clients'. A 2017 analysis of 77,000 UK job adverts by Totaljobs revealed 'lead' to be the most common male-gendered word used in job specs, while 'support' was the most-used female-gendered word.[5]

Review the words used in your job titles to ensure they are not mislabelling the role in a way that makes it sound more attractive for a man. When companies change job titles from technician to 'customer service technician' or from engineer to 'design engineer', more women apply.

All images and messaging used in recruitment marketing materials should portray the company and role in a way that would resonate with women and not reinforce stereotypical views. Use authentic images of diverse female employees on adverts and ensure your outreach activities feature diverse women. Always gain permission from your employees to use them for this purpose. I noticed a spate of posts on social media by black female students complaining that their image was used without consent, and their college's attempts to promote themselves as inclusive spectacularly backfired when some of these women claimed to have been subject to racism and sexism at university.

Be proud of and promote your remote and flexible working practices and maternity and parental leave policies in your recruitment. They're seen as an indicator of inclusion and are cited by women (and men) as a key reason to choose an employer. A 2015 PwC study of female millennials asked if an employer's policy on diversity, equality and workforce inclusion was important when deciding whether or not to work for them. The responses showed that 86% of women agreed and 74% of men. Young talent will only make a decision after exploring the diversity of the employer's leadership teams, understanding its diversity demographics and establishing what its diversity targets are.[6]

The following case studies feature companies which have put considerable effort into ensuring that they have robust recruitment and selection processes in place to avoid discrimination, and also developing a reputation for being an inclusive employer of choice.

Case study: Auto Trader Group plc

Auto Trader's aim is to lead the digital future of the UK automotive marketplace, and to meet that challenge they know that having a diverse workforce and an inclusive culture is vital. Their company values are embedded in all that they do, and their 'Community Minded' value underpins respect for diversity and advocating inclusion, and making a positive difference to the communities around them.

The company's leaders believe that having an inclusive culture and promoting themselves authentically as an inclusive employer has attracted a more diverse and gender-balanced talent pool of higher calibre. One way they achieve this is through supporting diverse routes into technology roles through their partnership with Tech Returners in Manchester. This is a development programme designed to bring beginners and returners to a job-ready level through teaching full-stack web development combined with career and personal development. Eighty per cent of the returners are women, helping to increase the numbers of women in STEM careers. Fantastic initiatives like this are fundamental to give women the technical skills to pursue a career in tech.

Auto Trader have a gender-balanced shortlist policy, train recruiters in diversity and inclusion and follow a structured interview scheme with behaviours and positive indicators. If any of their recruiters are not hiring a gender-balanced group of recruits, they must explain why not to the senior management.

All new starters participate in one-day workshops focusing on creating a common understanding of diversity and inclusion as well as exploring participants' unconscious biases and how they can impact their own behaviour and relationships with other people. They also meet the employee networks and are advised on how they can be actively involved in delivering the strategy. The workshop invitation is extended to customers and partners who take some of the learnings back to their own organizations.

Case study: Jardine Motors Group

To be able to attract talent, Jardine Motors Group believe that a business needs a strong brand profile and strong employee value proposition. They believe they've achieved both.

They've collaborated with a wide range of partners to support their diversity and inclusion strategy so it has credibility. Such partners include the Automotive 30% Club, Stonewall, Whizz-Kidz, Armed Forces Transition Programme, Women Ahead, Retail Week's Be Inspired initiative and the Valuable 500.

As well as undertaking outreach activities with schools and colleges to promote careers in their company and sector, they've implemented inclusive recruitment campaigns proactively targeting women to apply for roles, ensuring the messaging and imagery is inclusive and gender balanced, and that bias is removed from the recruitment and interview process through the use of a technology platform that engages candidates in a virtual and innovative way rather than just using a CV.

They recognize and celebrate their female talent so that it's clear that they're proud to be an inclusive employer of many successful women. In 2019, they had many colleagues recognized in Autocar's Top 100 Great British Women Rising Stars and the Automotive 30% Club Inspiring Automotive Women Awards. Jardine Motors Group also publishes Inspiring Stories on their social media platforms, an initiative which recognizes and celebrates rising talent, and profiles those with interesting and different career stories.

Summary

Ensuring person specifications and leadership traits aren't stereotypically male, using language and imagery to appeal to women, removing bias in the selection process, having gender-balanced shortlists and hiring in group cohorts will all lead to higher numbers of female recruits. The next step is to make sure there are no unfair impediments to their progression, and we will cover this in the following chapter.

13 Step 5: Pull women through the pipeline – Promote proportionately

After having recruited women into your organization and recalibrated the culture, structure and processes to ensure they're made welcome and included, you must turn attention to ensuring that women can progress through the skills pipeline up the management levels to the top of the organization. This will mean redesigning work allocation and promotion processes to remove subjectivity where bias could creep in.

In order to ensure your gender balance improves in the higher levels, it all boils down to making sure you promote proportionately. For example, if your entry level is 50% female and 50% male and your recruitment standards demand the same performance level of both, then your promotions to first level of management should also reflect this balance. If more men are being promoted than women then you have a problem somewhere in your processes or promotion criteria. We know that getting to the first rung of the management ladder is critical for women to progress, so it's essential that women don't leak from the pipeline at that stage. To ensure you promote proportionately to top levels, you must ensure that you have a large enough representation of women in the key roles up the management ladder that are seen as the stepping stones to executive committee and board roles.

To promote proportionately, the following will need to be addressed:

o   Remote and flexible working at the top

o   Succession planning

o   Ask her to apply

o   Coaching and leadership programmes

o   Sponsoring and mentoring

o   Women's networks

Remote and flexible working at the top

Most companies have flexible working policies that are mainly aimed at young mothers in junior roles. For many, it's unthinkable that a senior executive would have any working pattern other than being switched on 24/7. However, now more people want to work flexibly as they climb the career ladder, and it's becoming common for people to secure senior roles in their 30s and 40s who belong to a generation that places importance on work–life balance for myriad reasons.

Ensuring men and women can work flexibly irrespective of seniority will have a huge impact on the number of women who are able to progress through the company, and if men also work flexibly it will not be seen as a woman's issue.

Timewise, a flexible working consultancy in the UK launched the Timewise Power 50 to celebrate senior executives who work part-time. In 2020, the list includes both men and women in roles such as Global Director of Business Operations at Accenture, Chief Innovation Officer at EY and Head of Product – In Store Customer Transactions at Tesco. The majority have a four-day (or 80% to reflect agile working) contract, with others on a three-day or 60% contract.

Many of these people have been promoted internally from another part-time role. Some have been hired in, replacing a full-time incumbent. It's arguably better to have a top performer for 80% of the time than to have a mediocre performer 100% of the time, and it could make them more affordable to employ.

As remote and agile working becomes more popular, we may see more women choosing that instead of reduced hours. Often the reason for working a day less was to avoid the commute, and so be able to do the school run, or do some domestic tasks. As agile remote working becomes common practice, women and men can do this in the time they would have been wasting on the commute.

Inclusive leaders set a good example by adopting contemporary working patterns themselves, and encouraging their senior executive team to do the same.

Succession planning

I've always been surprised by the lack of succession planning in most companies. To build inclusive teams of complementary skills, it's essential to plan the moves of employees in advance of vacancies arising. It's a good practice that forces senior executives to get to know the strengths of direct reports and those at least a level below that, and also identifies skills gaps that in the future will need to be filled through training or external hires. It avoids incorrect assumptions being made about women's career ambitions.

For effective succession planning, you must future your organizational structure by at least five years, and plan the transition to your new gender-balanced teams. You need to track employees' time on position and identify their personal route to at least the next move. To be able to identify who will fit best where, formal sponsoring programmes involving the top team and structures like personnel development committees should be established. Employees should be consulted about their career plans and suggestions for alternative routes presented. Never let people assume they are next in line for a certain job, because they'll feel overlooked if they don't get it.

When I worked for Ford, they had a great process called 'Next Up'. Individuals were put forward by their sponsor and assessed without a job in mind to determine if they were ready for promotion. If successful, their name was put on the 'next up' list until the next vacancy round. The domino effect of internal moves always led to multiple vacancies at a particular level, and those on the list were interviewed for all roles. The candidates were slotted into the job that was the best fit. This process served to remove intense competition for a single job and enabled candidates to have an abundancy mindset. They may not have won their favoured role but they ended up with one they were best suited for, and they accepted that the other person was a better match. This process reduced aggressive competition between employees, and the team-oriented culture directed the employees' competitive behaviour against external threats instead.

Ask her to apply

The most common reason cited to me by leaders as to why they have a gender imbalance is that women don't apply for promotions. Coming into play is no doubt the Hewlett Packard 60% versus 100% phenomenon, where women feel they don't meet enough of the criteria. This can be tackled by simply asking them to apply because you know that they do.

There's also evidence that because women analyse what promotions will entail for them and their families, they expect similar positive outcomes but also much stronger negative outcomes from promotion than men do. They weigh up the pros and cons more. These women see high-level positions as equally attainable as their male peers but much less desirable. To overcome this, you must ensure women are given full and accurate information to base their decisions on rather than assumptions or hearsay. It should be coupled with exploring what the woman thinks makes the job undesirable, and either addressing misplaced concerns or reviewing the role to ensure that the best person for the job isn't unnecessarily excluded.

Coaching and leadership programmes

Both men and women benefit from development programmes. However, the critical issue is what is actually taught on them. For decades, women have been attending leadership training that has been primarily designed around stereotypically male attributes. What's needed now is training for everyone that champions more stereotypically female attributes, but also levels the playing field with regard to some traits. Some people (mainly but not all women) need to own their achievements and be more vocal and visible so that others are aware of their abilities. Some people (mainly but not all men) need to learn to include others and collaborate more and compete with peers less for the benefit of the business.

Coaching programmes tailored to the needs of specific groups are ultimately the most successful, and women and men tend to perform better in predominantly female cohorts. Combining leadership training with mentoring leads to more successful outcomes, because the delegate can talk through what she's learned and the mentor can see how much she has developed.

Sponsoring and mentoring

I've already covered the difference between the two and the importance of implementing official schemes in Chapter 6. I believe that official sponsorship programmes should be mandatory for all to participate in, whereas mentoring programmes should be mandatory for senior leader mentors, but voluntary for mentees. Many women think they need mentoring when they actually need a sponsor, so tend to be over-mentored and under-sponsored, with the reverse happening for men. In their 2010 *Harvard Business Review* article, Herminia Ibarra, Nancy Carter and Christine Silva cite a 2008 study that found that more women have mentors than men, and their relationship is based on the mentor helping them to develop their skills. Yet men have more senior mentors who are less likely to coach them on their weaknesses, and more likely to be an advocate in networks and make connections for them, and thus actually are acting as an unofficial sponsor.

This leads to a more successful outcome for the man than the woman.[1]

Women's networks

Networks for women can be extremely useful if they have a defined purpose. They broadly fall into two categories: networks founded by women as a way of connecting and supporting each other; or networks that are established as a business policy, that are explicitly inclusive to all, and have the purpose of providing suggestions and feedback as to what organizational changes would be beneficial to achieve a gender balance.

Both purposes are valid, but the former can flounder if they also wish to influence company policy because there is no one in a position of power to listen to them.

There's strong evidence that women's networks and conferences with a goal of inspiring, developing and supporting women have a significant positive impact on women's progression. This is aligned to the fact that women learn better in a female-heavy environment, as well as meet many female real models whose career path they can aspire to. Achor wrote in the *Harvard Business Review* in 2018 about his study with Gielan of 2,600 women attending Conferences for Women in the US. They examined outcomes that occurred in the year after the conference. The likelihood of receiving a promotion doubled for the attendees, and 15% of the women received a pay increase compared to only 5% of the non-attending control group. According to Laurie Dalton White, founder of the Conferences for Women:

> *Something special happens when you see that you are not alone. Making connections and building relationships with other attendees and speakers helps women form an understanding of their worth, and then they learn strategies to ask for promotions, seek fair pay, and even become mentors to others.*[2]

A company serious about being gender balanced should establish a gender-balance network that is inclusive for both sexes. The purpose is to share perspectives, find common ground and work together on solutions that are fed back to senior leadership for action. Male members learn that they're the other half of the gender balance and that they will also benefit from changes. Involvement should be encouraged, and led from the top.

In addition, companies should encourage and pay for female employees to join external women's networks and attend their conferences for inspiration and motivation from women in other companies who have successfully navigated their way to the top. Organizations with a predominantly male workforce could also establish a subgroup of their gender-balance network that acts as a friendship group for women across the company to get to know each other, connect and support each other. If you're the only woman in a particular group, it's useful to connect with women from other teams so you no longer feel you're a minority; you're part of something bigger. This is of particular value to young women in apprentice or junior roles.

Encourage women to join business and trade networks that are currently male dominated. Senior leaders who are unable to attend meetings should delegate their place to a woman. Business networks must do more to invite women to be speakers and attendees, and male leaders should refuse to appear on all-male panels so that the organizers look a bit harder for the invisible women.

The two case studies that follow show how Toyota GB and Marshall Motor Holdings are providing expert coaching in a female-only group setting to women in their companies.

Case study: Toyota GB

Toyota GB currently has 12.5% (one of eight) female representation on the UK-based executive committee and 18% in the direct report group. According to their 2019 gender pay gap report, they have 17.6% women in the upper pay quartile, 24.3% in the upper-middle quartile, 31.1% in the lower-middle quartile and 71.6% in the lowest-paid quartile. The company is committed to achieve at least 30% of key leadership roles to be filled by women by 2030.

Toyota GB management identified that the majority of women they employed are in the lower levels of the organization. Their Women in Business group (40 women from all levels) were asked what support they could be given to thrive at Toyota. Their responses reflected that the women were less comfortable with self-promotion and more likely to admit what they couldn't do than celebrate what they could. Despite performing well, many of them felt they lacked confidence and were affected by imposter syndrome.

On the premise that this reluctance to acknowledge their own performance and potential could hinder their progression, a personal development programme called 'Women on the Verge' was developed to help address it, with a focus on owning and changing the conversation about the woman herself, identifying what she wants to be and believing she could be it. The purpose of the development support was not to try to 'fix the women' so they could progress within the current Toyota culture; it was to enable them to fully and realistically appreciate their own talent and abilities, and be able to articulate them and be comfortable in making them more visible. The programme content emphasized the importance that Toyota places on inclusion of women at all levels of the organization.

Women on the Verge is an intimate workshop designed for a small-group female-only setting. Through conversation, the participants look at tools for managing perception with critical audiences, building the woman's own brand and reputation management campaign, cultivating confidence that comes from within, and building emotional resilience and mental toughness. The session provides an empowering environment where individuals explore the challenges and opportunities that being a woman at work brings, and helps them build the confidence and support to move further towards their own goals.

The programme was designed and developed by IDology Partnership, a coaching consultancy with decades of experience working with high-potential women all over the world. IDology's philosophy is grounded in an exploration of individuality and what it means to 'just be yourself'.

After seven workshops with 47 women attending, it's having a lasting impact on the participants. They've recommended it to others and have created their own social network, continuing to build on the relationships created in the sessions. The fact that participants came from all areas and levels of the organization has already improved communications and links across the business and increased the visibility of those attending.

More women are asking to attend future workshops and so Toyota has extended the programme, and will also be adding a sustainment workshop for the initial participants to review how they're progressing and to look at how they as a group can support other women and share their learning.

Every newly promoted person at Toyota GB is assigned a trained coach from the management group for a period of 90 days to help them to quickly settle in. All employees can request a coach if they feel it will be of benefit. For three years, Toyota GB have also participated in the Women Ahead Global 30% Club cross-company mentoring scheme, through which over 30 women have been mentored by senior executives from other sectors, and the same number of Toyota leaders have been mentors to women from other companies.

Case study: Marshall Motor Holdings plc

Marshall Motor Holdings employs 3,746 people in 126 dealership locations across the UK, and represents 26 manufacturer franchises. The CEO, Daksh Gupta, is a Patron of the Automotive 30% Club and has made a commitment to implement the club's 30 by 30 strategy. The company currently has 43% female representation on the board (three of seven), and 17% female representation on the executive committee (one of six). According to their 2019 gender pay gap report, 14.4% of those in the highest-paid quartile are women, 17.9% in the upper-mid quartile, 32.4% in the lower-mid quartile and 33.8% in the lowest-paid quartile.

Marshall Motors identified that a key priority was to take action to remove barriers to progression their female staff might be facing, to address the lower levels of female representation in the middle and higher management levels of the company. As a result of an introduction via the Automotive 30% Club, the company participated in a pilot programme developed by executive coach Julia Philpott, called Advanced 250.

It's a unique programme of group coaching sessions, in a small-group setting, specifically for women based on research that a woman's experience in the workplace is different to a man's, especially in traditionally male-oriented environments such as the automotive sector. The executive team selected six women in management roles across the business to participate. The group were a mixture of head office specialists and front-line operators from their dealership network.

In addition to their commitment to help address the gender imbalance across the sector, Marshall Motors felt the key elements of this programme covered some of the amplified challenges that women face in business versus men. It included learning about overcoming the imposter phenomenon, and being aware that high performance and popularity are negatively correlated for women, but positively correlated for men. It also showed that women face a 'potential penalty', in that employers find it hard to assess a woman's potential as she is often a trailblazer in that space, so she will often be asked to 'prove it again' with a lateral move (which she will often accept) whereas a man will not. The company leadership wanted to establish if this programme was something they could add to the personal development of Marshall women in management roles.

The six participants found it hugely valuable, gaining a greater understanding of the psychology of why men and women are different, and the stereotypes of 'bossy' and 'over-emotional'. They also learned how to develop enhanced coaching skills. What was even more impactful is that the group realized they all faced similar challenges, and now have a network of trusted confidants that will be sustained. One of the participants has since been promoted.

HR Director Jo Moxon notes: 'The spotlighting and group coaching sessions were incredibly powerful and gave everyone an understanding of their strengths and achievements but also what may be holding them back. The real success factor of the sessions was based on the initial scene setting that created a trusted environment for everyone to feel comfortable to be themselves.'

The women reported an improvement in self-recognition and confidence. Some stated they felt the business was already reaping the results of their development. They felt reassured that they didn't need to emulate their male counterparts and that their way of managing colleagues and situations is just as valid. One participant commented: 'Marshall will benefit hugely from this programme in terms of helping our women to understand the value they bring to the business and increase their self-awareness. The group sessions create a feeling of solidarity and empowerment and I saw people grow in confidence through the process. It is also a great way to improve coaching skills and understand our impact on people based on how we behave. The relationships that are built as part of this process will prove invaluable going forward. The concept of all of our female managers having a network of trusted support is very exciting!'

Summary

There are many actions that organizations can take to pull women through the promotional pipeline. Pay them the same as men and be transparent about it; see them as diverse women, some of whom happen to be mothers; put programmes in place to sponsor, coach and mentor them; establish gender-balance networks and encourage women to join business and women's networks; and ask them to apply for promotions. Check if you're promoting proportionately; if not, you must identify what's stopping it.

These actions will also help you to retain women, and we will explore other issues that must be addressed to stem a leaking female talent pipeline in the next step.

14 Step 6: Hold on to your investment – Maintain the balance

Having invested considerable resources in recruiting and promoting women, make sure you don't lose them before you get the return on that investment. Study your people analytics to establish not only the actual overall male and female turnover rates in your business, but also where specifically the differences might be happening. Is it in the lower levels, or in certain teams, or in particular jobs? If the data shows a disproportionate number of female or ethnic minority employees are leaving, then there's a problem.

The previously mentioned 2015 PwC report on female millennials cites the top five reasons that young women then aged 25 to 40 left their roles. Number one was not enough opportunities for career progression; followed by the work not being interesting and meaningful enough; insufficient learning and development opportunities; better pay; and an imbalance between work effort and compensation.[1]

It's evident that taking action in these areas is critical to keep women in the organization. There are also other factors below the surface that may not have been covered by the PwC report. Women may leave organizations due to a lack of appreciation, being side lined after maternity or because of sexual harassment and abuse.

Here are some of the issues to address to make sure you hold on to the investment you have made in your female employees:

o   The motherhood penalty

o   The career slow lane

o   Successful women are unpopular

o   Fixing women to fit

o   Harassment and hostility

o   Fair and equal pay

o   Work–life overload

o   Allocate work fairly

o   Credit and recognition

The motherhood penalty

It's usually a joint decision to become parents, yet women face a motherhood career penalty and men have the advantage of a fatherhood premium. Generous maternity policies giving many months paid leave to mothers but only two weeks statutory paid paternity leave to fathers (and less than two-thirds actually take the full entitlement) immediately force gendered roles on each parent. Due to the gender pay gap, in most cases the woman will stay home because the household takes less of a financial hit. This gives men an immediate advantage in the workplace; they don't have a gap on their CV, they don't miss out on promotions and they're not viewed as having a reduced commitment to the company. Often a mother can't get back on the career ladder.

The introduction of shared parental leave in England, Scotland and Wales is a positive step forward. It enables parents to share between them up to 50 weeks, of which 37 weeks are entitled to statutory pay, and of which the mother must take at least two weeks. However, take up of parental leave by men is low because as well as the financial penalty there's a culture in many workplaces that attaches a stigma to men who choose to care. This data, along with the gender split of who works flexibly and remotely, is a critical indicator of the gender stereotypes that exist in your organization.

The real way to fix the motherhood penalty is to provide fully paid parental leave to men and women, and make remote, flexible or part-time working available to all. The default should be that all employees take their full leave entitlement, and are praised for it. This is a sound investment because these policies attract talent, reduce the gender pay gap (it widens when only women take time out), generate loyalty amongst all employees and normalize that men and women can both be carers and have careers.

Accenture offer 36 weeks' paid leave to mothers and fathers, and the Managing Director, Mark Smith, set a good example when he took seven months off to look after his son. Etsy, Aviva and most recently Fidelity all now provide 26 weeks' parental leave on full basic pay to all employees. In 2019, Diageo announced that all parents employed by them in the UK are eligible for 52 weeks' parental leave, with the first 26 weeks fully paid regardless of gender or how they became a parent. It is open to 4,500 employees, of which 3,100 are in manufacturing roles. Several senior men have taken up the policy and are sharing their experiences to encourage others and to challenge cultural norms around paternity leave.

Don't conflate all women with mothers while ignoring that many men are fathers. There's still a reluctance to hire women due to the cost of maternity leave and fear of a reduced level of commitment. The thinking is: 'Women will have babies and will choose to care for them. Men may father babies but will not choose to care for them.' This assumes free choice on behalf of men and women, when in fact the expectations of society and policies and systems driven by such stereotypes effectively eliminate free career and parenting choices.

Some women will never become mothers. 2018 Office for National Statistics figures reveal that 19% of women at the age of 45 have no children (although some may adopt or care for the children of others). Those that do will only face balancing childcare and career for around a third of their working life.

Ensuring that all policies to attract and retain women only revolve around caring responsibilities associated with young children is a mistake.

So not all women are mothers and not all men are breadwinners, and parenthood doesn't define a worker or their value. Equal parental leave and flexible working policies can level the playing field and remove a career advantage for men and replace it with a carer benefit equal to women. It can actually be a win-win for both sexes: neither is negatively affected by caring for their child or fall behind on the career ladder.

The career slow lane

'Prove it again' is a phenomenon whereby women must prove they are already competent at the level of a job, whereas men are promoted on future potential. Due to a lack of female role models at senior levels, there's an assumption that a man will be able to step up, but a woman is a higher risk. So even if a woman is ready, her supervisor or promotional panel may think her similarly competent male peer is a better bet. Being overlooked or turned down for promotion will make that woman look elsewhere, so check this isn't happening in your business.

Don't put women returners in the career slow lane, with 'pay protected' demotions, sideways moves to less important roles, or removal from succession plans. This is a discriminatory practice that happens in many organizations because decisions are made about the woman without consulting her, or assumptions are made about how motherhood will have impacted on her performance and commitment so she must be removed from any business-critical roles. This is often linked to returning on a flexible working pattern; the company creates a discriminatory situation by only allowing certain less important roles to be done flexibly so the woman returner is forced to go into a slow-lane job. Avoid this by opening up most jobs to flexible working, and enabling part-timers to be promoted. If you have a high-performing woman returner, it will benefit your business to ensure she continues in a business-critical role. If you won't, she will leave and find a company that will.

Successful women are unpopular

Another reason women might leave is that the more successful they become, the less liked they are by both men and women. Success and popularity are positively correlated for men yet negatively correlated for women. This impacts on peer reviews, promotion and popularity of senior women, and can ultimately lead to their exit.

This was proven in the famous 'Heidi-Howard' experiment. Professor Frank Flynn of Columbia University experimented with gender perceptions using a case study about Heidi Roizen, a successful Silicon Valley entrepreneur who maintained a wide professional network and leveraged it to the benefit of herself and others. While teaching the Roizen case to mixed-sex classes, Flynn changed Heidi's name to Howard in some versions. He measured the students' reaction and found more said they would enjoy working with Howard than Heidi. The students who thought the protagonist was a woman thought she was more aggressive, and disliked her more. Students said they found Heidi less humble, and more power hungry and self-promoting than Howard. All students thought Heidi and Howard were equally competent, but Howard was seen as more likeable whereas Heidi was seen as selfish and not the type of person you would want to hire or work for. This held true for both male and female students.

Most companies hire and promote against a set of leadership traits that have been created by identifying common characteristics of successful leaders. However, the data will be skewed to being male, because there are few female leaders. This results in us thinking that leaders must display stereotypically masculine traits to be successful. So when we try to assess a woman against these leadership traits, she is often a poor match. If a woman does reflect these characteristics, she is successful, but we dislike her because it causes dissonance with our views of what a woman should be like. This caused the unpopularity of Heidi Roizen; she demonstrated leadership traits that in the minds of the students were male.

Redesigning the desired leadership traits to include a gender-balanced complementary mix of stereotypically 'masculine' and 'feminine' characteristics, and looking for leaders to embody them all, will help overcome the difference in popularity and acceptance of successful women, and also lead to the inclusion of a more diverse group of men. It is this mix of traits that makes inclusive leaders successful.

Fixing women to fit

Much of the gender-balance movement has focused on fitting women into a traditional masculine culture and structure. Sheryl Sandberg, COO of Facebook, famously encouraged women to 'lean in'. Companies will encourage women to attend leadership training, to learn to lead more like men. Actually, they don't need training more than men do; they are as effective, but many will tend to lead differently.

Inclusive leaders understand that gender balance is the result of conscious design and adaptation, not squeezing women into male-normed organizations. Avivah Wittenberg-Cox, author and CEO of the gender-balance consultancy 20-first, in an article for *Talent Quarterly*, suggests that leaders of gender-balanced firms know that:

> ... the best leadership is a balance of masculine and feminine energies and people. They discourage 'alpha male' behaviours in both men and women and seek to create corporate cultures that are 'gender bilingual' rather than normed to whichever group runs the place (usually men).[2]

Women are not less capable leaders, and shouldn't need to either 'man up' to fit in or have to ship out.

Harassment and hostility

Hostile working environments are another reason for leaving. The Equality Act 2010 defines sexual harassment as 'unwanted conduct of a sexual nature' which violates dignity or 'creating an intimidating, hostile, degrading, humiliating or offensive environment'.[3] The House of Commons Women and Equalities Committee report on *Sexual Harassment in the Workplace* states:

A wide range of behaviour can come under this definition: sexual jokes or comments, remarks about someone's body or appearance, displays of pornographic material, cat calls or wolf-whistling, flashing, sexual advances, groping, sexual assault, or rape.[4]

The common factors are the effect that the conduct has on the victim, and that it is unwanted.

It's hard to determine the scale of the issue within particular organizations, because most women don't report the harassment; they simply leave. A ComRes poll for BBC Radio 5 Live in 2017 found that 53% of women and 20% of men said they had experienced sexual harassment at work or a place of study, and one in ten of the women who had been harassed said they had been sexually assaulted.[5]

The Women and Equalities Committee report draws a correlation between sexist behaviour and inequality in the culture of an organization, stating that:

… sexual harassment can be considered both a cause and consequence of sex inequality, and some of the evidence we received drew links between sexual harassment and other manifestations of gender inequality in the workplace such as the gender pay gap and the underrepresentation of women in leadership roles.[6]

Those who stay and endure it may suffer damage to their mental and physical health, and are unlikely to perform to their potential or progress with their careers. Some men use sexual harassment as power against women to prevent them from effectively competing. Women who have suffered workplace abuse describe changing their behaviour as a result, wearing different clothes, shoes that they could run away in, and missing breaks to avoid sitting with male colleagues passing round pornographic images on their phones.

Young women, disabled people or members of sexual minority groups are more likely to suffer, along with workers in precarious employment contracts. These people are viewed as weaker with less power, and less likely to be listened to or valued by the business over the perpetrator. The vast majority of perpetrators are men, harassing both women and men. If young women or minority groups are leaving a particular area of your organization, this could be why.

Fair and equal pay

Women want to be paid what they believe their efforts are worth, and expect to be paid the same as men. Unfortunately, that doesn't always happen, and can be a reason for them leaving. The 1970 Equal Pay Act prohibited less favourable treatment between men and women in the UK in terms of pay and conditions of employment. The Act and subsequent amendment in 1984 list three principles: equal pay for the same work; equal pay for work of equal value; and equal pay for work rated as equivalent. The Equality Act of 2010 gives a right to equal pay between women and men for equal work. The Act requires a sex equality clause to be automatically inserted into all contracts of employment, ensuring that a woman's contractual terms are no less favourable than a man's.

It's a fact, however, that men are still being paid more than women for doing the same job. Headline-hitting examples are in the media world, where bosses pay male stars more because they claim they appeal to a bigger audience. Presenter Samira Ahmed won the employment tribunal she brought against the BBC, claiming she was underpaid for hosting audience feedback show *Newswatch* at £440 an episode compared with Jeremy Vine's salary of £3,000 per episode for *Points of View*. The BBC failed to prove the pay difference was not because of sex discrimination. The BBC's main argument was that Vine was a famous entertainer, and they had to pay him a high rate to prevent him from going to a competitor. The tribunal found the actual skills needed for his show were that of a journalist like Ahmed's and that as it was fully scripted there was no extra talent being brought by Vine. Therefore, it was Vine that was being unfairly overpaid for a job that didn't warrant it.

In most businesses, men and women are paid the same for exactly the same job. A deeper discussion should be had about whether an HR director is of equal value or does equal work to a sales director. In stereotypically female roles such as HR, the pay is usually less than stereotypically male roles such as sales and you should explore further if that is acceptable. If you pay market rates for both roles, even though you're aware that they're equally as critical to the business, you will likely end up with your female HR director earning significantly less than your male sales director. You will perpetuate the gender pay gap within your company.

You must examine your pay policy and ensure you're meeting the legal requirements. If it isn't transparent, why are the facts hidden? The answer is likely to be that there is unfairness in the system that will lead to some employees realizing they have been treated inequitably. Transparency is essential for trust and to prove equity and equality. Women are emboldened to ask what their pay is relative to others, and male allies, often surprised to hear about the gap, are telling them what their salary package is. If there's a big gap, women may leave.

Work–life overload

One often-cited reason for leaving is that women have so much work to do when they get home that they're in effect putting in a third shift. Sometimes this is overwhelming, and because it's not possible to give the children back, or easy to exchange the husband for a more considerate model, it's the job that goes. This is certainly a common excuse made by women in exit interviews, because it doesn't burn any bridges by laying blame at the door of the employer. If genuine, the woman doesn't pop up in a similar job elsewhere within a few months (keep an eye on LinkedIn).

To tackle this, explore if she's being overwhelmed because of misplaced perceptions about the requirements of the job. Does she really need to be in the office every day? Does she need to travel for that meeting or can it be done on video call? Is she delegating as much as her male peers, and does she have as many people to delegate to? Is she being given unpaid tasks on top of the day job when male colleagues are not?

If you don't want to lose out on reaping the optimum rewards from the investment you've made in her, investigate if you can come to an agreement with regard to her work pattern that would enable her to reduce workload, even if it's as simple as working remotely and saving travel time.

Allocate work fairly

High-profile accounts and projects are often subjectively allocated and given visibility, and usually given to men, while women are given less exciting or more difficult tasks. Women are therefore perceived as not performing as well as male peers, and any prejudiced assumption that they're not as good is reaffirmed. A 2012 study by Janice Madden in two US brokerage firms found evidence for such performance-support bias, in that women were generally assigned inferior accounts. However, it also found that women produce sales equivalent to men if given accounts with equivalent prior sales histories.[7]

You must make sure work is fairly and equitably distributed to avoid such performance-support bias. This may mean redesigning the process through which people are allocated work tasks to ensure it's more objective. Women will leave if they're repeatedly given the short straw.

Credit and recognition

We must celebrate successful women and give them visibility. If she feels her efforts are going unnoticed or she's being taken advantage of, she may become demotivated and leave, particularly if she's also underpaid. Women may claim they're not given sufficient recognition for their ideas and efforts because male peers and supervisors are quick to take the credit. Every woman can cite an example, most likely when working alone in a group of men. It's not by accident that the phrase is 'success has many fathers'.

There are a number of reasons for this. Women are often more softly spoken than men, so when they voice an idea in a meeting and no one hears it, a man will often 'hepeat' it but not give credit to the woman. Sometimes this is intentional;

but apparently not always – my husband often thinks a little voice in his head piped up with the idea and truly thinks it's his and not mine. Microphones can help in large meetings, and with the adoption of video conferencing women are apparently being heard more easily.

Many female scientists and academic researchers have had their work taken by men and presented as their own. A notorious example is that of Watson and Crick who won the Nobel Prize in 1962 for the Watson-Crick DNA double helix they named, but in fact Rosalind Franklin of King's College discovered it in 1951. In the contemporary world of work, women claim that papers and reports submitted to higher management have their names removed, or they're missed off congratulatory emails to give the impression to others that they weren't involved.

Perpetrators do this to both men and women, but more often get away with it with women who don't challenge them publicly. I know a male executive who created a sales programme that had a significant impact. When he moved to a senior role in another company, he started recruiting and a few male managers from the original company applied. He was entertained when each one laid claim to the creation of that sales programme. He took great pleasure in pointing out their dishonesty, and that a bit of research could have saved them from humiliation.

To prevent women leaving due to a lack of recognition, create a climate in which senior leaders are truth seekers with regard to who is really making what contribution, enabling women to challenge the idea stealers without suffering retribution. Also create mechanisms through which people are encouraged to reveal the great work their female peers are doing, such as supporting external awards that recognize their contribution.

Case study: Vertu Motors plc

Robert Forrester, the CEO of the large motor retailing group Vertu and member of the Automotive 30% Club, announced at an industry conference that he had introduced a policy of firing on the grounds of gross misconduct for proven sexual harassment. He admitted that in the past, like most other businesses in the sector, if the man had been a top performer he would probably have simply been disciplined. Now though he understood that the real damage such men were doing to female colleagues, the overall business and the culture was far greater than any positive contribution they were making. By implementing this policy of zero tolerance, it sent a clear message to other potential perpetrators. This statement was powerful to hear not only because it had clearly been implemented unwaveringly in his organization, but also because he was prepared to make it public to his industry peers. After the conference, other senior male leaders told me that this zero-tolerance approach would be upheld in their businesses with immediate effect.

Case study: JCT600 Ltd

JCT600 Ltd, an automotive retailer with 48 car dealerships throughout Yorkshire, Derbyshire, Lincolnshire and the North East, is one of the many member companies of the Automotive 30% Club. In 2019, the club launched the inaugural Inspiring Automotive Women Awards to recognize and celebrate women who are an inspiration to their colleagues, no matter where they work in their business. Women are nominated for the award by their peers rather than by senior leadership, and the employees of JCT600 came out in force to nominate 41 of their female team members. Before the winners were announced, the JCT600 HR Director, Katie Saunders, asked for the full list of the women nominated in their company. She took the step of writing to each one to congratulate them on being nominated because it showed what an inspiration they were to their peers internally, which was as important to the company leadership as the external recognition that any winner would have.

This simple yet wonderfully emotionally intelligent act of revealing to the women that they had been nominated by their work colleagues led to huge positive feedback from them, indicating how motivated and proud they felt, and how it was so meaningful to know their team members felt they were inspirational.

When the final winners were announced, they included four women from JCT600, including Katie Saunders, and a young Ferrari vehicle technician who also worked on race track events was given a special recognition Trailblazer Award for being a pioneer in her role.

So it is essential to look for ways to celebrate and appreciate the contribution of women in your business to motivate them to progress and also to engender loyalty, and this can be through both internal recognition and external awards.

JCT600 have also taken an inclusive leadership stance by making it clear that sexual harassment will not be tolerated. This followed an incredibly imaginative approach to communicating the negative impact of such incivility to the top team, through creating a short film that shared with them the real-life experiences of what some women had endured in their workplaces, but performed by senior JCT600 female executives. The powerful message of real events coupled with realizing it could be happening to women like their colleagues led to immediate action.

Summary

Diverse women are a valuable resource. Without them, you can't achieve a gender-balanced diverse business, and you will lose out on the profit gains it brings. By examining why women leave, and specifically where from, and addressing those factors in your organization you are more likely to retain talented women. It's also important to invest in ways to motivate and retain all good performers.

The final chapter will explain that the person driving the business transformation described throughout this book needs to be you, and will reveal why now is the time for you to become a game-changing leader.

Part 3 If not you, then who? If not now, when?

15 Be a game-changing leader: Leave a lasting legacy

Have I managed to convince you that building a gender-balanced inclusive business is not only the right thing to do for your business, your customers and your employees, but it is also the right thing for society? Now you are aware that inequity, inequality and exclusion really do exist, you might be thinking: 'Why doesn't someone *do* something about this?' That someone should be you. Perpetuating the status quo in your organization and missing out on the benefits that an inclusive culture brings is not a wise thing to do. Doing nothing to change it is not really an option. With power comes responsibility to act.

But have I outlined a compelling enough argument to motivate you to personally want to act, and to do it now? Do you want to be a game-changing leader?

Many leaders are acting now to radically transform their businesses to be more adaptable, agile and responsive, embracing new technologies and employing the best people. They are trailblazers, pioneers amongst their peers, and will reap the benefits first. They are intellectually curious, quick to adapt, always learning, consulting people to tap into their collective intelligence and ensuring no one is excluded. If you are like them, then you are displaying inclusive leadership traits and you should get started on the journey to building a winning gender-balanced business.

Leading an inclusive organization requires you to lead by example and inspire others to change their individual behaviour and group norms. This change will transform your business and wider society for the better, and could achieve an amazingly positive impact, leaving a legacy for generations to come.

Leading such a radical business transformation by redesigning your organizational processes, systems and protocols to suit the diverse 21st-century worker of both sexes is truly game changing. Identifying and upholding the social values that will make your company the one that people aspire to join and will thrive in will take you to the forefront of the next industrial revolution: when companies acknowledge that their profits and destinies are inextricably interwoven with the quality of life and success of those around them in wider society.

We are on the brink of a 'Fifth Industrial Revolution' in which trust will be earned by those companies that apply the Fourth Industrial Revolution technologies to improving the state of the world. This signals that we are likely to experience another seismic shift; the existing and future global technology giants will realize the value of having social responsibility and refocus their purpose to include doing what society needs; probably driven by their customers' and their own employees' desire to add value to society. Join that revolution.

According to Alan Mulally, ex-CEO of Ford Motor Company and Boeing, and Doug Ready in their 2017 MIT Sloan Management Review article, game changers are purpose-driven, performance-focused and principles-led.[1] Does that sound like you? They suggest that to be a game-changing leader, you need to craft a compelling change story, emphasizing the importance of a gender-balanced organization, and get buy-in from your entire organization so there is a powerful sense of ownership and accountability. They also recommend you balance the need to 'express a sense of urgency about driving change, with the patience it will take to do things well and right at a deliberate pace, signalling that it takes time to effect tangible, sustainable results'.

To change the game and reap the business benefits of gender balance and diversity, you must set the example and lead from the top, and make the creation of diverse gender-balanced teams a strategic and operational priority throughout the organization, monitoring progress with key metrics and asking high-quality questions to determine the validity of the results.

Hold your team and their reports collectively accountable for building an inclusive culture and delivering the goals, and reward inclusive leadership behaviour. Have change agents, advocates, allies and role models at all levels in the business and insist on collaboration and cooperation across diverse teams. Show zero tolerance for sexual harassment, be staunchly anti-sexist, anti-racist and anti-homophobic.

Create talent-management processes that ensure that you will have the necessary pipeline of diverse women to accomplish your aims, and coach and drive exceptional performance, while removing under performers. Scan the environment for complementary skills and acquire talented women from competitors.

In Chapter 8, I talked about finding your purpose, your raison d'etre that helps you to lead a meaningful and fulfilling life. You are at the reins of your organization. You may have founded the company or are the current steward of its success and direction, and you must build its reputation and legacy by being a bold catalyst for change. It's what you love doing, it's what you are good at, it's what you get paid for, and building a winning gender-balanced diverse business is definitely what society needs. It may lead you to achieving the sense of fulfilment that is your Ikigai.

An aspect of Ikigai is living by 'Ichi-Go Ichi-E', knowledge that this moment exists only now and won't happen again. You can't catch it back and you may regret not using it to the max and squeezing every last drop out of it.

Now is the time for you to change the game. Marc Benioff summarizes:

I firmly believe that in the future, equality will be the key to unlocking a company's full and sustainable value. That doesn't mean it's easy to achieve. But those who fail to try will be on the wrong side of history.[2]

So be on the right side of history, and follow the route map to building a winning gender-balanced business by implementing the Six Steps to Success, and start to change the game.

Further resources

30% Club
https://30percentclub.org
The 100% Club
https://the100percentclub.co.uk
Automotive 30% Club
www.automotive30club.co.uk
Business in the Community
www.bitc.org.uk
Education and Employers
www.educationandemployers.org
Equality and Human Rights Commission
https://equalityhumanrights.com
The Fatherhood Project
www.thefatherhoodproject.org
Fawcett Society
www.fawcettsociety.org.uk
Global Institute for Women's Leadership, King's College London
www.kcl.ac.uk/giwl

Hampton-Alexander Review, FTSE Women Leaders

https://ftsewomenleaders.com

HeForShe

www.heforshe.org

Inclusive CEOs

www.inclusiveceos.com

Moving Ahead

https://moving-ahead.org

Parity.org

www.parity.org

Victim Support

www.victimsupport.org.uk

Women and Equalities Committee

https://committees.parliament.uk/committee/328/women-and-equalities-committee

Women in Business Network

www.wibn.co.uk

Women Returners

https://womenreturners.com

Women's Business Council

http://womensbusinesscouncil.co.uk

Working Mums Ltd

www.workingmums.co.uk

Acknowledgements

I must thank many people for encouraging me to write the book that my teachers predicted would emerge one day.

This would not have happened without my kind friend from my Sheffield High School days, Vicki Capstick, who heard my regret expressed in an interview with Radio Sheffield that I had not fulfilled this promise to those teachers. She connected me with the wonderful Alison Jones of Practical Inspiration Publishing who thought it was worthy of a publishing deal.

I would like to express my gratitude to the brilliant Patrons of the Automotive 30% Club – Daksh Gupta, Astrid Fontaine, Kristian Elvefors, Catherine Faiers and Stuart Miles – and also club members Robert Forrester, Rachel Shepherd, Clare Wright, Amanda Mogan-Wilson, Neil Williamson, Alex Smith, Penny Weatherup, John Tordoff and Katie Saunders for providing me with such rich case studies and also for their continued enthusiastic support of the campaign. Also special thanks go to Nathan Coe, CEO of Auto Trader Group plc, for writing the Foreword, and Paul Van Der Burgh for being the very first member of the club and being a sponsor, advocate and ally of mine throughout my career.

I must express thanks to my fantastic Gaia Innovation team who held the fort to enable me to finally finish the book, the hugely supportive 30% Club Global Steering Committee members, and the powerhouse in female form that is Roz Bird, Commercial Director of MEPC and Chair of the Silverstone

Technology cluster, for being such a strong supporter of equality and who 'lifts others as she rises'.

Finally, my thanks go to my mum, dad and brother who have always been proud of what I do, and my wonderful family James, Kate, Alex and Will, who not only believed without question that I could actually deliver this book, but also gave me the space to immerse myself in writing during lockdown, James tempting me out occasionally with a glass of rosé on a warm summer evening. My children are my inspiration; they motivate me to take action now to ensure things will change for them in the workplace, and their natural instinct for inclusion and to fight sexism, racism and homophobia enables me to firmly believe that there is hope that future generations will achieve gender and racial parity. An extra special thanks goes to my daughter Kate for her valuable insight and amazing support. She has the strength, courage, determination and conviction that inspires me and others to fight exclusion and build a fair and socially just future. She and her peers will finish what we start and will truly change the game.

Endnotes

Introduction

[1] McKinsey Global Institute, *UK Power of Parity: Advancing Women's Equality in the United Kingdom*, May 2017.

Chapter 1 The business benefits of balance: Don't settle for less

[1] Marc Benioff, *Trailblazer: The Power of Business as the Greatest Platform for Change*, 2019, p. 1.

[2] 30% Club, 'Our ethos', https://30percentclub.org/about/who-we-are

[3] McKinsey & Company, *Diversity Wins: How Inclusion Matters*, May 2020.

[4] Peter Dizikes, 'Workplace diversity can help the bottom line', *MIT News*, 7 October 2014, citing Sarah Ellison's article, 'Diversity, social goods provision and performance in the firm'.

[5] MSCI, *The Tipping Point: Women on Boards and Financial Performance*, 13 December 2016.

[6] Michelle McSweeney, '10 companies around the world that are embracing diversity in a BIG way', *Social Talent*, 7 August 2016.

[7] Global 30% Club and PwC, *Are You Missing Millions? The Commercial Imperative for Putting a Gender Lens on Your Business*, November 2019.

[8] Different Spin – Good Rebels, *Mad Maxine: Does Automotive Fail Women?* February 2016.

[9] Hive, *State of the Workplace Report*, 2018.

[10] Boston Consulting Group report by Rocio Lorenzo, Nicole Voigt, Mike Tsusaka, Matt Krentz and Katie Abouzahr, *How Diverse Leadership Teams Boost Innovation*, 23 January 2018.

[11] Sylvia Ann Hewlett, Melinda Marshall and Laura Sherbin, 'How diversity can drive innovation', *Harvard Business Review*, 2 August 2013.

[12] Glassdoor, *What Job Seekers Really Think About Your Diversity and Inclusion Stats*, 17 November 2014.

[13] PwC, *Winning the Fight for Female Talent: How to Gain the Diversity Edge Through Inclusive Recruitment*, March 2017.

[14] Stephen Turban, Dan Wu and Letian Zhang, 'When gender diversity makes firms more productive', *Harvard Business Review*, 11 February 2019.

[15] Deloitte, *Millennial Survey*, May 2018.

[16] Deloitte, *Millennial Survey*, June 2020.

[17] CMI report by Roger Steare, Pavlos Stamboulides, Peter Neville Lewis, Lysbeth Plas, Petra Wilton and Patrick Woodman, *Managers and the Moral DNA: Better Values, Better Business*, March 2014.

[18] Hampton-Alexander Review report, November 2019, p. 43.

Chapter 2 Inclusive leadership: Create a winning business

[1] Nathan Coe, 'Inclusive Talks' video interview for InclusiveCEOs.com, July 2020.

[2] Business in the Community report by Dr Gillian Shapiro, of Shapiro Consulting Ltd, and Helen Wells and Rachael Saunders of Opportunity Now, *Inclusive Leadership from Pioneer to Mainstream – Maximising the Potential of Your People*, September 2011.

[3] Marc Benioff, *Trailblazer: The Power of Business as the Greatest Platform for Change*, 2019, p. 118.

[4] Marc Benioff, *Trailblazer: The Power of Business as the Greatest Platform for Change*, 2019, p. 102.

[5] Yorkshire Tea, Twitter post, 8 June 2020, https://twitter.com/yorkshiretea/status/1270047023669133316

[6] The Diversity Practice, *Different Women Different Places*, 2007.

7 Joep Hofhuis, Pernill G.A. van der Rijt and Martin Vlug, 'Diversity climate enhances work outcomes through trust and openness in workgroup communication', *SpringerPlus*, 5, Article number 714, June 2016.

8 Frank Dobbin and Alexandra Kalev, 'Why doesn't diversity training work? The challenge for industry and academia', *Anthropology Now*, September 2018.

9 Nathan Coe, 'Inclusive Talks' video interview for InclusiveCEOs.com, July 2020.

Chapter 3 A burning platform: Now is the time

1 PwC, *Annual Global CEO Survey*, January 2017.

Chapter 4 Slaying the dragon of positive discrimination: Dispelling myths and creating legends

1 Tom Schuller, *The Paula Principle: How and Why Women Work Below Their Level of Competence*, 2017.

2 Black Business Awards, *The Middle: Progressing Black Asian and Ethnic Minority Talent in the Workplace Through Collaborative Action*, 2017, p. 44.

3 Parker Review, *Ethnic Diversity Enriching Business Leadership*, February 2020, p. 23.

4 Michael Kimmel, *The Gendered Society*, 2007, p. 191.

Chapter 5 Overcoming barriers and handling resistance: Inspire, inform and reform

1 Michael Kimmel, *The Gendered Society*, 2007, p. 191.

2 Black Business Awards, *The Middle: Progressing Black Asian and Ethnic Minority Talent in the Workplace Through Collaborative Action*, 2017, p. 23.

3 Richard Thaler and Cass Sunstein, *Nudge: Improving Decisions About Health, Wealth and Happiness*, 2008.

Chapter 6 What men can do: Sponsors, advocates, mentors and allies

[1] Archbishop Emeritus Desmond M. Tutu, 'Let us measure up as men', Skoll World Forum, Skoll.org website, November 2012.

[2] Rosie Campbell, *Hampton-Alexander Review* report, 2019, p. 24.

[3] Warren Buffett, 'Warren Buffet is bullish ... on women', *Fortune* magazine, May 2013.

Chapter 7 What women can do: Trailblazers, real models, growers and lifters

[1] Madeleine Albright speech, New Hampshire, reported by Tom McCarthy in *The Guardian*, 6 February 2016.

[2] Caroline Hoxby, *Peer Effects in the Classroom: Learning from Gender and Race Variation*, NBER Working Paper, August 2000.

[3] Brad Barber and Terrance Odean, 'Boys will be boys: Gender, overconfidence and common stock investment', *Quarterly Journal of Economics*, 2001, 261–292.

[4] Tara Sophie Mohr, 'Why women don't apply for jobs unless they're 100% qualified', *Harvard Business Review*, 25 August 2014.

[5] Laura McInerney, 'British girls have finally made the global top table ... for fear of failure. How terrifying', *The Guardian*, 17 December 2019.

Chapter 8 Find your purpose and reason for being: The wider impact on the world

[1] Marc Winn, Ikigai Venn diagram, *What's Your Ikigai? The View Inside Me*, 14 May 2014, http://theviewinside.me/what-is-your-ikigai/

[2] Marc Benioff, *Trailblazer: The Power of Business as the Greatest Platform for Change*, 2019, p. 21.

[3] Education and Employers, *It's Who You Meet: Why Employer Contacts at School Make a Difference to the Employment Prospects of Young Adults*, 2012.

[4] Education and Employers, *Motivated to Achieve*, 2019.

[5] McKinsey & Company, *The Power of Parity*, 2017.

[6] Margaret Mead, in *La Abogada* newsletter, by the International Federation of Women Lawyers, Vol. 3 (1967), p. 5.

[7] Eirini Flouri, *Fathering and Child Outcomes*, 2005.

[8] Karin Grossmann, Klaus Grossmann, Elisabeth Fremmer-Bombik, Heinz Kindler, Hermann Scheuerer-Englisch and Peter Zimmerman, 'The uniqueness of the child–father attachment relationship: Fathers' sensitive and challenging play as a pivotal variable in a 16-year longitudinal study', *Social Development*, 11(3), 301–337 (2002).

[9] Paul Amato, 'Father–child relations, mother–child relations, and offspring psychological well-being in early adulthood', *Journal of Marriage and Family*, November 1994.

Chapter 9 Step 1: Know your data – Be accountable for progress

[1] Office for National Statistics, 'Gender pay gap in the UK: 2019', Office for National Statistics website (http://ons.gov.uk), 29 October 2019.

[2] Rosabeth Moss Kanter, 'Some effects of proportions on group life: Skewed sex ratios and responses to token women', *American Journal of Sociology*, 82(5), 965–990 (1977).

[3] Sir John Parker, *A Report into the Ethnic Diversity of UK Boards*, the Parker Review Committee Final Report, 12 October 2017, p. 48.

[4] '5 Whys: The Ultimate Root Cause Analysis Tool', www.kanbanize.com

Chapter 10 Step 2: Reach out to new talent pools – Find new sources of skills

[1] Marc Benioff, *Trailblazer: The Power of Business as the Greatest Platform for Change*, 2019, p. 108.

[2] PwC, *The Female Millennial: A New Era of Talent*, 2015.

[3] PwC, *Women Returners: The £1 Billion Career Break Penalty for Professional Women*, 2016.

Chapter 11 Step 3: Recalibrate for inclusion – Design for productivity not presenteeism

[1] Joost Van Hoof, 'Female thermal demand', *Nature Climate Change*, 5, 1029–1030 (2015).

[2] Tom Chang and Agne Kajackaite, 'Battle for the thermostat: Gender and the effect of temperature on cognitive performance', PLOS ONE, 14(5), e0216362 (2019).

[3] PwC, *Winning the Fight for Female Talent*, 2017.

[4] Justin Lavelle, 'Gartner CFO survey reveals 74% intend to shift some employees to remote work permanently', Gartner.com website, July 2020.

[5] Cebr report for Citrix, *The Potential Economic Impacts of a Flexible Working Culture*, August 2019.

[6] One-Poll survey for Citrix, 'Remote work: The new normal?' Citrix.com website, April 2020.

[7] Titan Alon, Matthias Doepke, Jane Olmstead-Rumsey and Michèle Tertilt, *The Impact of COVID-19 on Gender Equality*, National Bureau of Economic Research (NEBR), April 2020.

[8] Uwe Jirjahn and Gesine Stephan, 'Gender, piece rates and wages: Evidence from matched employer–employee data', *Cambridge Journal of Economics*, 28(5), 683–704 (2004).

[9] Jeffrey Flory, Andreas Leibbrandt and John List, *Do Competitive Workplaces Deter Female Workers? A Large-Scale Natural Field Experiment on Gender Differences in Job-Entry Decisions*, National Bureau of Economic Research (NEBR), November 2010.

[10] Uri Gneezy, Kenneth Leonard and John List, 'Gender differences in competition: Evidence from a matrilineal and a patriarchal society', *Econometrica*, 77(5), 1637–1664 (2009).

[11] John Coates, *The Hour Between Dog and Wolf*, 2012.

Chapter 12 Step 4: Welcome in the women – Recruit equitably

[1] Benjamin Artz, Amanda H. Goodall and Andrew J. Oswald, 'Do women ask?' *Warwick Economics Research Papers*, July 2016.

[2] Stephanie Johnson, David Hekman and Elsa Chan, 'If there's only one woman in your candidate pool, there's statistically no chance she'll be hired', *Harvard Business Review*, April 2016.

3 Iain Moss, 'Gender bias in job ads: How job ads reinforce the gender pay gap', Adzuna.co.uk website, February 2019.

4 Danielle Gaucher, Justin Friesen and Aaron C. Kay, 'Evidence that gendered wording in job advertisements exists and sustains gender inequality', *Journal of Personality and Social Psychology*, 101(1), 109–128 (2011).

5 Joshua Murray-Nevill, 'How UK job ads bias applicants by gender', Totaljobs.com website, November 2017.

6 PwC, *The Female Millennial: A New Era of Talent*, September 2015.

Chapter 13 Step 5: Pull women through the pipeline – Promote proportionately

1 Herminia Ibarra, Nancy Carter and Christine Silva, 'Why men still get more promotions than women', *Harvard Business Review*, September 2010.

2 Shawn Achor, 'Do women's networking events move the needle on equality?' *Harvard Business Review*, February 2018.

Chapter 14 Step 6: Hold on to your investment – Maintain the balance

1 PwC, *The Female Millennial: A New Era of Talent*, September 2015.

2 Avivah Wittenberg-Cox, '5 gender balance myths most men still believe', Talent-Quarterly.com website, March 2020.

3 Equality Act 2010, Section 26, www.legislation.gov.uk/ukpga/2010/15/section/26

4 House of Commons Women and Equalities Committee report, *Sexual Harassment in the Workplace*, Fifth Report of Session, 2017–19, July 2018, p. 4.

5 ComRes survey for BBC Radio 5 Live, 'Sexual harassment in the workplace survey', ComResGlobal.com website, October 2017.

6 House of Commons Women and Equalities Committee report, *Sexual Harassment in the Workplace*, Fifth Report of Session, 2017–19, July 2018, p. 7.

7 Janice Madden, 'Performance-support bias and the gender pay gap among stockbrokers', *Gender and Society*, 26(3), 488–518 (2012).

Chapter 15 Be a game-changing leader: Leave a lasting legacy

[1] Doug Ready and Alan Mulally, 'How to become a game-changing leader', *MIT Sloan Management Review*, September 2017.

[2] Marc Benioff, *Trailblazer: The Power of Business as the Greatest Platform for Change*, 2019, p. 119.

'This eye-opening book will leave you questioning why the pace of change is so slow when the benefits are so clear. The evidence speaks for itself, and this is a must-have read for any business leader.'

Stuart Miles,
MD, CDK Global (UK) Ltd

'Change the Game is full of practical steps to help leaders drive better gender balance. There is no quick fix but for any leader looking to make progress, this is a great place to start.'

Catherine Faiers,
COO, Auto Trader Group plc

'In a male-dominated sector, few have done more to highlight the automotive sector's lack of progress in getting an appropriate gender balance in the workforce than Julia. The book makes for uncomfortable reading and shows the work to be done.'

Robert Forrester,
CEO, Vertu Motors plc

'A timely read given the pandemic. This book gives a real-world approach to tackling gender balance in the workplace – I encourage all leaders to read it and take note.'

James Brearley,
CEO, Inchcape UK

'This is a great example of a book that provides practical execution-oriented advice from the start. Evidence led, it creates a route through some of the most challenging parts including how to pitch to the unconvinced and how to systemically make changes. If every organization worked with the six steps, we could make real progress to level the playing field.'

Sarah Morris,
Group Chief People Officer, Compass Group plc

'Forget the box-ticking. Forget the endless parade of statistics. Forget "blaming the women". This guide cuts through years of jargon and posturing to the heart of what it takes to reach gender equality.'

M. Tamara Box,
Managing Partner, EME at Reed Smith LLP and passionate gender-balance campaigner